A gift for

Mother

Presented by

Tom & Jan

Treasury of *Joy* and Inspiration

Our Most Moving Stories Ever

The Reader's Digest Association
New York, NY / Montreal

A READER'S DIGEST BOOK

Copyright © 2013 The Reader's Digest Association, Inc.

The credits that appear on pages 315–318 are hereby made part of this copyright page.

Library of Congress Cataloging-in-Publication Data

The Reader's digest treasury of joy & inspiration : our most moving stories ever / the editors of Reader's digest.
    p. cm.
 "A Reader's digest book."
 ISBN 978-1-62145-049-8 (alk. paper)
 1. Inspiration--Literary collections. I. Reader's Digest Association.
PN6071.I6R43 2013
808.8'0353--dc23

                    2012029040

We are committed to both the quality of our products and the service we provide to our customers. We value your comments, so please feel free to contact us.

> The Reader's Digest Association, Inc.
> Adult Trade Publishing
> 44 South Broadway
> White Plains, NY 10601

For more Reader's Digest products and information, visit our website:

> www.rd.com (in the United States)
> www.readersdigest.ca (in Canada)

Printed in the United States of America

1 3 5 7 9 10 8 6 4 2

Contents

Introduction

BY LIZ VACCARIELLO, EDITOR-IN-CHIEF

OW DO you distill 90 years of beloved articles (shelves and shelves of bound editions housed in a mansion-like library) into a single sparkling volume that you can hold in your palm?

When we decided to celebrate our 90th anniversary by publishing a book of our best stories, it felt like trying to squeeze the Colorado River into a bottle of Coke. Then I reframed the question: How does the brand that made its name by "curating and condensing" the best reads in the land curate and condense itself?

Because that is one skill that *Reader's Digest* editors have shared across generations and decades and anniversaries: the ability to select those stories that are so moving, so evocative, so honest, and so bold that they change your perspective on life. That vision, brought to life in 1922 by founders Dewitt and Lila Wallace, is the mission we still carry on today. And we have the unique privilege of acting on the feeling that such stories inspire: *Everyone should read this. This story must be shared.*

So I'm indebted to this team of editors who spent weekends and late nights reading through our archives to select the best of *Reader's Digest*—these "reads of lasting interest." Many selections moved us to tears; others made us laugh until we forgot our worries. Some are written by the thought leaders of their time—such as Dwight D. Eisenhower, who expresses in a way that no one else can why all students should go to college. Others celebrate the indelible mark left by longtime contributors such as Alex Haley, the Pulitzer Prize–winning author of *Roots,* and Fulton Oursler, a prolific author and senior editor of *Reader's Digest* from 1944 to 1952. Inside you'll find famous and not-so-famous names, selected and reprinted from newspapers, magazines, books, radio broadcasts, and television specials.

The media we curate from have changed, but the nature of our choices has not. Our selections evoke what we call the extraordinary ordinary: the bond of family, the gift that can change a life, the love of a pet, the quiet coincidences that can be directed only by a divine hand.

The editors who participated in this project told me they felt changed after reading through their trove of *Reader's Digest* articles. Because that's the power of a great story: It lifts our spirits, teaches us something new, connects us to our community, and inspires us with ideas about who we might become. It's my sincere wish that you experience the same feeling from reading this *Reader's Digest* treasury.

L. Vaccariello

Joy
Joy
Joy

Overtaken by Joy

April 1965

T WAS a day in late June, gray and depressing, with clouds hanging low. My husband and I were driving to Nova Scotia, Canada, for a much needed vacation, both of us more tired than we cared to admit. We traveled glumly, hoping to reach rest and dinner before the rain came. Suddenly, on a lonely stretch of highway flanked by woods, the storm struck. The forest vanished in a great deluge. Cascades of water shut us in, making driving impossible. We pulled off onto the shoulder of the road and stopped.

Then, as though someone had turned off a celestial faucet, it ended. A thin radiance, like a spray of gold, spread out from the clouds, catching the top of the trees. Every blade of grass was crystalline as the sun flashed on trembling drops. The very road shone. And then a rainbow arched across the sky. But more than that: on our right was a pond, and in the pond was the end of the rainbow! It was as though this arch of living color had been built for us alone. We could hardly speak for awe and joy.

A friend of mine has described a similar experience. She had walked out on a lonely beach at twilight. It was a time of grief for her, and loneliness was what she wanted. Offshore, across the darkening sea, was a single low island. Presently she was aware of a dim light moving on the island, and then came the splash of oars and the scrape of a boat leaving the shore. She made out the outlines of a fishing boat, and in it the figure of a man. He rowed a little way and anchored. My friend told me that, after a while, she felt an intense and glowing sense of oneness with that silent figure. It was as though sea and sky and night and those two solitary human beings were united in a kind of profound identity. "I was overtaken by joy," she said.

MOST OF us have experienced such lighted moments, when we seem to understand ourselves and the world and, for a single instant, know the loveliness of living beings. But these moments vanish quickly, and we are almost embarrassed to admit that they have ever been, as though in doing so we betray a willingness to believe in what is not true.

However, psychologist Abraham Maslow of Brandeis University embarked some years ago on a study of average, healthy individuals and found that a great many report such experiences—"moments of great awe; moments of the most intense happiness or even rapture, ecstasy or bliss." He has concluded that these experiences are often the expression of buoyant health.

In his files, for example, is the story of a young mother. Getting breakfast for her family, she hurried about the kitchen pouring orange juice and coffee, spreading jam on toast. The children were chattering; the sun streamed in on their faces; her husband was playing with the littlest one. All was usual. But as she looked at them, she was suddenly so overcome by how much she loved them, by her feelings of good fortune, that she could scarcely speak for joy.

Here, too, is the story of a man who remembers a day when he went swimming alone and recalls "the crazy, childish joy with which he cavorted in the water like a fish." He was so overwhelmed by his great happiness at being "so perfectly physical" that he shouted again and again with joy.

Apparently almost anything may serve as the impetus of such joy—starshine on new snow; a sudden field of daffodils; a moment in marriage when hand reaches out to hand in the realization that this other person speaks as you speak, feels as you feel. Joy may wait, too, just beyond danger when you have enough to face a situation and live it out. It may come from such a simple thing as waking in the night on a train as it pulls into a station, hearing voices calling to one another out of the darkness, seeing a face smiling warmly in the light of the trainman's lantern. Whatever the source, such experiences provide the most memorable moments of human life.

Joy is much more than happiness. It is "exultation of spirit," says the dictionary, "gladness; delight; a state of felicity." Awe and a sense of mystery are part of it; so are the feelings of humility and gratitude. Suddenly we are keenly aware of every living thing—every leaf, every flower, every cloud, the mayfly hovering over the pond, the crow cawing in the tree-top. "O world, I cannot hold thee close enough!" cried the poet Edna St. Vincent Millay in such a moment.

Enthralled, we see as we never saw before. The most important thing in these peak experiences, says Professor Maslow, is the feeling of these people that they had really glimpsed "the essence of things, the secret of life, as if veils had been pulled aside."

We see, too, the unity of things—a dazzling vision of the kinship we all have with one another and with the universal life around us. Everyone who has ever had such a moment has noted this quality of "melting into." There is a feeling that life is a whole; I and my world are part of each other; I and all life are united in a bond of love and understanding. And we feel free to be ourselves. Suddenly we know who we are and what we are meant to be. All doubts, fears, inhibitions, tensions and weaknesses are left behind. This is our true self and we have found it.

"To miss the joy is to miss all," wrote Robert Louis Stevenson. For these moments of joy are like flowers in the pastureland of living; or like a plough turning up the gasping earth in a dry and weed-bound field. Life grows larger, we draw deeper breaths, doors open softly within us. "Where there is joy, there is fulfillment," wrote Paul Tillich in *The Meaning of Joy*, "and where there is fulfillment, there is joy."

THE SAD thing is that it happens to most of us so rarely. As we grow older, our lives become buried under the pressures of the workaday world. Joy is not likely to come to us when we are going round and round the tormenting circle of our own busyness, and our own importance.

What we need is the child's spontaneity and wonder of discovery. "To me every hour of the light and dark is a miracle," wrote Walt Whitman. And English naturalist Richard Jefferies, desperately poor and fighting a deadly disease, could cry from his invalid's chair, "Every blade of grass was mine as if I had myself planted it. All the grasses were my pets: I loved them all. Every wild hawk that passed overhead was mine. What more beautiful than the sweep and curve of his going through the azure sky? Oh, happy, happy days! So beautiful to watch; and all mine!"

How can we restore to our lives this eager openness to all the world which is so often the prelude to joy? Sometimes all that is needed is a chance to see an old experience in a new way. I remember one such occasion. I had been working all night on a manuscript. It would not come right, and I felt I could never finish it. But as the clock struck five, the last sentence fell into place and I put down my pen, opened the door and stepped out into the lawn. The stars were thinning out and the sky in the east had that "light-is-coming" look. A few birds began to sing, tentatively trying out their voices, each seemingly waking the next. The trees, dark shapes on the horizon, began now to take on form and configuration. A streamer of light caught the weeping willow across the street and sharply etched one branch of our birch tree. The sky lightened all along the eastern horizon. More trees appeared, one by one. The great maples lighted with brilliance like candelabra in the dark.

The sun was up! There was a golden blaze behind the dark trees, a quickened freshness in the air. Twig by twig the sun set fire to every branch and leaf. The birds now were singing wildly as though they had just been created by the morning itself; and I, too, felt newly created, so full of joy that it seemed I could not hold it.

Most of us need to learn to break out of the prison of self. For joy comes not only from fusion with nature; it comes from love and creativeness; from insight and discovery and great emotion. Perhaps joy is most likely to come when we forget ourselves in service, or in the pursuit of a great dream. Florence Nightingale, working long, hard hours to become a nurse, could say "This is life! I wish for no other world than this!"

HANDEL WROTE his *Messiah* in a little more than three weeks. Working morning, noon and night, he hardly touched the food set before him. When he had finished Part Two, which contains the "Hallelujah Chorus," he rushed to the window weeping with joy, and his servant heard him cry, "I did think I did see all heaven before me and the great God Himself!"

Most of all, joy may come when we do not run from life—from its sorrows, its struggles and its hopes. The person who wants above all to avoid risk and danger and sufferings sets out no welcome for the moments of joy.

When life's transiency and frailty are omnipresent, what we have grows sweeter. As G. K. Chesterton said, "The way to love anything is to realize that it might be lost."

I remember finding myself seated beside an old gentleman on a train some years ago. He sat quietly looking out of the window. His eyes searched each leaf, each cloud, the lines of passing houses, the upturned faces of children watching the train go by.

"It is beautiful, isn't it?" I ventured at last, intrigued by his absorption.

"Yes," he said, and no more for a moment. Then he smiled and waved a hand at a passing hay wagon. "See," he said. "Hay going to the barn." And he made it sound as though there could be no greater event in all the world than a wagonload of hay on its way to the mow.

He saw the unspoken question in my face. "You think it's strange," he said, "that just a hay wagon means so much. But you see last week the doctor told me that I have only three months to live. Ever since, everything has looked so beautiful, so important to me. You can't imagine how beautiful! I feel as if I had been asleep and had only just woken up."

PERHAPS WE are more likely to experience a moment of joy if we can admit that there is more to life than we have yet fathomed; if we can acknowledge a world greater than our own. To be sure, the experience of joy is not necessarily religious in any conventional way. But a distinguishing characteristic of joy is the feeling people have that they have touched the hem of something far beyond themselves.

In my own life there was a moment of this special exaltation. En route by plane to the Midwest, we were flying at a high altitude, and a continent of shining clouds spread beneath us. Often, before and since, I have watched these radiant towers and hillocks of cloud go by. But this time the scene was haunted by a strange joy so penetrating that the plane seemed not to be there.

I thought of myself as living and walking in a land like that, and I, who is the most gregarious of humans, knew in a flash of deep illumination that there was in the universe a light, a stuff, a tissue, a substance in company with which one would never be lonely. The experience left the compelling certainty that we dwell safely in a universe far more personal, far more human, far more tender than we are.

What if these moments of joy are given to us to reveal that this is the way we are meant to live? What if the clarity of joy is the way we should be seeing all the time? To many people, it seems almost wicked to feel this radiance in a world threatened as ours is. But most generations have known uncertainty and challenge and peril. The more grievous the world, the more we need to remember the luminous beauty at the center of life. Our moments of joy are proof that at the heart of darkness an unquenchable light shines. 🕊

Amen to That

A PREACHER was asking for contributions to the church's program to buy food for the needy. The town gambler, who also owned the saloon and several other shady operations, offered the preacher $500.

"You can't take that," a scandalized deacon told the preacher. "That's the devil's money."

"Well, brother," said the preacher, cheerfully accepting the gift, "in that case, the devil has had his hands on it long enough. Now let's see what the Lord will do with it."

James Dent

• • •

AS A NEW minister, I wanted my first holiday services to be both attractive and meaningful. The Christmas eve service included a candle-lighting ceremony in which each congregant lit a candle from his neighbor's candle. At the conclusion of the ceremony, the congregation sat hushed, pondering the beauty of the moment. I rose to announce a hymn and was taken completely by surprise when laughter broke out in response to my invitation: "Now that everyone is lit, let's sing 'Joy to the World.'"

Shall We Dance?

BY NEIL SIMON

September 1999

FROM *The Play Goes On*

SOMETIME AFTER the opening of *The Sunshine Boys* and George Burns's winning of the Oscar, my then-wife, Marsha Mason, threw a 50th-birthday party for me in Beverly Hills. There were about a hundred guests, and my mother sat at our table. She was looking at the far end of the room where George Burns was sitting with his costar, Walter Matthau.

In one of my plays, there is a scene where the mother tells her son about the night she danced with actor George Raft when she was a young girl. That scene was based on a story my mother had told me over and over again.

When she was 16, living in the Bronx, Mamie Levy (my mom) was known as one of the best ballroom dancers in the neighborhood. A fellow would have to be pretty light-footed on the dance floor to have the nerve to ask her for a spin around the room. One night, a young George Burns, who was better known then for his fox-trots and tangos than he was for his comedy, dropped in.

In my play I used the name of George Raft instead of George Burns, since a Latin Lover made the story more provocative. But it was George Burns who spied her on the floor that night and chose her as his dancing partner for the better part of the evening. The next day, Mamie Levy was the talk of the east Bronx. Overnight she had become, at least in that small corner of the world, a star.

My mother played and replayed that glorious night in her life, telling it to me over and over again from the time I was seven through my entire childhood. I'd nod each time and say, "Gee, that's great, Mom."

And each time she'd say, "You don't believe me."

Now it was almost 60 years later, and she was in the same room with George Burns again. I knew this was an opportunity not to be missed. I said, "Mom, come with me. I want to introduce you to George."

To my surprise, she declined. "No, I'd be embarrassed. He'd never remember me."

"Well, you could remind him," I said.

"No, it's all right. Besides, you never believed that story."

I felt frustrated but didn't push it. Twenty minutes later, George started to make his way around the room to take a few bows for his Academy Award. With the ever-present cigar in hand, he stopped to say hello to everyone and never left a table before he got a big laugh.

A six-piece orchestra was playing and people started to get up to dance. I watched my mother's eyes as she watched George moving closer to where we were sitting. When he finally came over, he put his arm around my shoulder and said, "Keep up the good work, kid. Someday you'll make it." I laughed. My mother smiled politely.

Then he looked at her and said to me, "And who is this attractive lady, Neil?"

"George, this is my mother, May Simon," I told him.

She nodded, smiled and said, "How do you do?"

I assumed George would turn and move away to the next table. Instead he said, "Mrs. Simon, would you give me the honor of this dance?"

She didn't miss a beat. "I would love to," she said as she got up and was led away by George.

It was as if time had never passed. He moved her

gracefully across the hardwood floor, although he was now 81 and she was just a few years younger.

As I watched them, they didn't seem to exchange a word, their feet being more compatible than their conversation. Everyone was watching, sensing something special was happening, but not having a clue as to what.

They made their way toward our side of the room. I was praying the music would never stop. As they neared our table, George gave my mother a little spin. As his back was to our table, she looked at me and mouthed, "Now do you believe me?"

It is an indescribable moment when a son sees his mother getting the greatest thrill of her life. She handled it with grace and dignity. I could see she was overflowing with joy. The tears welled up in my eyes.

She never once said anything to George about that night almost 60 years before in a Bronx ballroom, and never repeated the story to me ever again. There was no need to. 🕊

All Creatures Great and Small

A TRUCK ran a red light, almost sideswiping our car. As my husband veered away, he threw his arm across me, protecting me from a possible collision. I was ready to plant a big kiss on my hero's cheek when he apologized.

In his haste, he admitted, he had forgotten it was me in the front seat and not our black Labrador, Checkers.

April Cole

The Bottom Line on Happiness

BY CLAYTON M. CHRISTENSEN

February 2011

EXCERPTED FROM *Harvard Business Review*

MY CLASS at Harvard Business School helps students understand what good management theory is and how it is built. In each session, we look at one company through the lenses of different theories, using them to explain how the company got into its situation and to examine what actions will yield the needed results. On the last day of class, I ask my students to turn those theoretical lenses on themselves to find answers to three questions: First, How can I be sure I'll be happy in my career? Second, How can I be sure my relationships with my spouse and my family will become an enduring source of happiness? Third, How can I be sure I'll stay out of jail? Though the last question sounds lighthearted, it's not. Two of the 32 people in my Rhodes Scholar class spent time in prison. Jeff Skilling of Enron fame was my classmate at Harvard Business School.

I graduated HBS in 1979, and over the years, I've seen more and more of my classmates come to reunions unhappy, divorced and alienated from their children. I can guarantee you that not a single one of them graduated with the deliberate strategy of getting divorced and raising children who would become estranged from them. And yet a shocking number unwittingly implemented that strategy. The reason? They didn't keep the purpose of their lives front and center.

Having a clear purpose has been essential to me. But it was something I had to think long and hard about before I understood it. When I was a Rhodes Scholar, I was in a very demanding academic program, trying to cram an extra year's worth of work into my time at Oxford. I decided to spend an hour every night reading, thinking and praying about why God put me on this earth. It was a very challenging commitment because every hour I spent doing that, I wasn't studying applied econometrics. I was conflicted about whether I could really afford to take time away from my studies, but I stuck with it and ultimately figured out the purpose of my life.

My purpose grew out of my religious faith, but faith isn't the only thing that gives people direction. For example, one of my former students decided that his purpose was to bring honesty and economic prosperity to his country and to raise children who were as capably committed to this cause, and to each other, as he was. His purpose is focused on family and others, as is mine.

Here are some management tools that can be used to help you lead a purposeful life.

1. Use your resources wisely.

YOUR DECISIONS about allocating your personal time, energy, and talent shape your life's strategy. I have a bunch of "businesses" that compete for these resources: I'm trying to have a rewarding relationship with my wife, raise great kids, contribute to my community, succeed in my career and contribute to my church. And I have exactly the same problem that a corporation does. I have a limited amount of time, energy and talent. How much do I devote to each of these pursuits?

Allocation choices can make your life turn out to be very different from what you intended. Sometimes that's good: Opportunities that you never planned for emerge. But if you don't invest your resources wisely, the outcome can be bad. As I think about my former classmates who inadvertently invested in lives of hollow unhappiness, I can't help believing that their troubles relate right back to a short-term perspective.

When people with a high need for achievement have an extra half hour of time or an extra ounce of energy, they'll unconsciously allocate it to activities that yield the most tangible accomplishments. Our careers provide the most concrete evidence that we're moving forward. You ship a product, finish a design, complete a presentation, close a sale, teach a class, publish a paper, get paid, get promoted. In contrast, investing time and energy in your relationships with your spouse and children typically doesn't offer that same immediate sense of achievement. Kids misbehave every day. It's really not until 20 years down the road that you can say, "I raised a good son or a good daughter." You can neglect your relationship with your spouse, and on a daily basis it doesn't seem as if things are deteriorating. People who are driven to excel have this unconscious propensity to underinvest in their families and overinvest in their careers, even though intimate and loving family relationships are the most powerful and enduring source of happiness.

If you study the root causes of business disasters, over and over you'll find this predisposition toward endeavors that offer immediate gratification. If you look at personal lives through that lens, you'll see the same stunning and sobering pattern: people allocating fewer and fewer resources to the things they would have once said mattered most.

2. Create a family culture.

IT'S ONE thing to see into the foggy future with acuity and chart the course corrections a company must make. But it's quite another to persuade employees to line up and work cooperatively to take the company in that new direction.

When there is little agreement, you have to use "power tools"—coercion, threats, punishment, and so on, to secure cooperation. But if employees' ways of working together succeed over and over, consensus begins to form. Ultimately, people don't even think about whether their way yields success. They embrace priorities and follow procedures by instinct and assumption rather than by explicit decision, which means that they've created a culture. Culture, in compelling but unspoken ways, dictates the proven, acceptable methods by which members of a group address recurrent problems. And culture defines the priority given to different types of problems. It can be a powerful management tool.

I use this model to address the question, How can I be sure my family becomes an enduring source of happiness? My students quickly see that the simplest way parents can elicit cooperation from children is to wield power tools. But there comes a point during the teen years when power tools no longer work. At that point, parents start wishing they had begun working with their children at a very young age to build a culture in which children instinctively behave respectfully toward one another, obey their parents and choose the right thing to do. Families have cultures, just as companies do. Those cultures can be built consciously or evolve inadvertently.

If you want your kids to have strong self-esteem and the confidence that they can solve hard problems, those qualities won't magically materialize in high school. You have to design them into your family's culture, and you have to think about this very early on. Like employees, children build self-esteem by doing things that are hard and learning what works.

3. Avoid "just this once."

WE'RE TAUGHT in finance and economics that in choosing investments, we should ignore sunk and fixed costs and instead base decisions on the marginal costs—that is, the price of each individual new step or purchase. But I teach that this practice biases companies toward using what they've already put in place— what helped them succeed in the past—instead of guiding them to create the capabilities they'll need in the future. If we knew the future would be exactly the same as the past, this would be fine. But if the future's different, and it almost always is, then it's the wrong thing to do.

The marginal cost doctrine addresses the third question I discuss with my students: how to live a life of integrity. Often when we need to choose between right and wrong, a voice in our head says, "Look, I know that as a general rule, most people shouldn't do this. But in this particular extenuating circumstance, just this once, it's okay." The marginal cost of doing something wrong "just this once" always seems alluringly low. It suckers you in, and you don't look at where that path is ultimately headed and at the full costs that the choice entails. Justification for infidelity and dishonesty in all their manifestations lies in the marginal cost economics of "just this once."

I'd like to share a story about how I came to understand the potential damage of "just this once" in my own life. I played on the Oxford University varsity basketball team. We worked our tails off and finished the season undefeated. The guys on the team were the best friends I've ever had in my life. We got to the British equivalent of the NCAA tournament and made it to the final four. It turned out the championship game was scheduled for a Sunday. I had made a personal commitment to God at age 16 that I would never play ball on Sunday. So I went to the coach and explained my problem. He was incredulous. My teammates were, too, because I was the starting center. Every one of the guys on the team came to me and said, "You've got to play. Can't you break the rule just this one time?" I'm a deeply religious man, so I went away and prayed about what I should do. I got a very clear feeling that I shouldn't break my commitment, so I didn't play in the championship game.

In many ways, that was a small decision, involving one of several thousand Sundays in my life. In theory, I could have crossed over the line just that one time and then never done it again. But looking back, I can see that resisting the temptation of "just this once" was one of the most important decisions I have ever made. My life has been an unending stream of extenuating circumstances. Had I crossed the line that one time, I would have done it over and over in the years that followed.

The lesson I learned is that it's easier to hold to your principles 100 percent of the time than it is to hold to them 98 percent of the time. If you give in to "just this once," based on a marginal cost analysis, as some of my former classmates did, you'll regret where you end up. You've got to define for yourself what you stand for and draw the line in a safe place.

4. Remember to be humble.

IT'S CRUCIAL to take a sense of humility into the world. If your attitude is that only smarter people have something to teach you, your learning opportunities will be very limited. But if you have a humble eagerness to learn something from everybody, your learning opportunities will be unlimited. Generally you can be humble only if you feel really good about yourself and want to help those around you feel really good about themselves too. When we see people acting in an abusive, arrogant, or demeaning manner toward others, their behavior almost always is a symptom of their lack of self-esteem. They need to put someone else down to feel good about themselves.

5. Choose the right yardstick.

DON'T WORRY about the level of individual prominence you have achieved; worry about the individuals you have helped become better people. This is my final recommendation: Think about the metric by which your life will be judged, and make a resolution to live every day so that in the end, your life will be judged a success.

All in a Day's Work

I HAD signed up to be a school volunteer and was helping a first-grader with her homework. But it turned out I was the one in need of help. The assignment required coloring, and I'm color-blind—can't tell blue from red. As we finished our lesson, I told the little girl, "Next week you can read to me."

Looking confused, she said, "Can't you read, either?"

Howard Sieplinga

Obey That
Impulse

BY WILLIAM MOULTON MARSTON

April 1941

CONDENSED FROM A CBS Radio Broadcast

FOR YEARS as a psychologist I have sought in the careers of great and of everyday people the inner springs that make for successful living. There are two which seem to me of prime importance: The first is hard work, governed by cool, logical thoughtfulness. The other is sudden, warm, impulsive action.

Admitting that I can't name a single person of true accomplishment who hasn't forged out of brains and hard work, I still hazard the sweeping assertion that most of the high spots and many of the lesser successes in their careers stem from *impulses* promptly turned into action.

Most of us actually stifle enough good impulses during the course of a day to change the current of our lives. These inner flashes of impulse light up the mind for an instant; then, contented in their after-glow, we lapse back into routine, feeing vaguely that sometime we might do something about it or that at least our intentions were good. In this we sin against the inner self, for impulses set up the lines of communication between the unconscious mind and daily action. Said William James, "Every time a resolve or fine flow of feeling evaporates without bearing fruit, it is worse than a chance lost; it works to hinder future emotions from taking the normal path of discharge." Thus we fail to build up the power to act in a firm and prompt and definite way upon the principal emergencies of life.

Once, in Hollywood, where Walter B. Pitkin and I were retained by a motion-picture studio, a young promoter presented an ambitious production idea to us. The plan appealed to both of us. It was, I thought, distinctly worth considering; we could think it over, discuss it and decide later what to do. But even while I was fumbling with the idea, Pitkin abruptly reached for the phone and began dictating a telegram to a Wall Street man he knew. It presented the idea in the enthusiasm of the moment. It carried conviction.

To my amazement, a ten-million-dollar underwriting of the picture project came as a result of that telegram. Had we delayed to talk it over we might have cautiously talked ourselves out of the whole idea. But Pitkin knew how to act on the spur of the moment. He had learned to trust his impulses.

Behind many an imposing executive desk sits a man who is there because he learned the same lesson. You've probably seen him in action more than once. Somebody is presenting to him a new idea, say in employe relations. It calls for extensive changes in office routine. And, deciding instantly, he calls an associate and gives instructions to make the change—then and there, not next week or next month.

We envy such men the ease with which they make up their minds and swing into action. But this ease is acquired over a long period of years. Rather than being, as we sometimes think, a privilege of their position, it is a practice that has led to their success. First in small matters and then in larger ones, they have acquired the do-it-now habit.

Calvin Coolidge remains an enigma to political commentators because the reasons for his actions were seldom apparent and the source of his astuteness could not be traced. No one could seem less impulsive than Coolidge, yet all his life he trained himself to rely on "hunches." He was not afraid of his impulses, and the celebrated Coolidge luck followed a pattern of action based on them. As a young attorney in a country law firm Coolidge was interviewing an important client one day when a telephone message informed him that the county political boss was in town. It occurred to Coolidge that he ought to see the local bigwig at once and propose himself as a candidate for the legislature. Without hesitation, this usually shy young lawyer cut his legal conference short, left the office and hunted up the county leader. That impulse bore fruit, and from then on the inner urges of Coolidge led him consistently to political success.

It should be clear from Coolidge's case that the person who follows his impulses is not necessarily flighty. The timid soul, however, is fearful lest impulse lead him into all manner of mistakes. But mistakes are inevitable—we are bound to make them no matter which course we take. Some of the worst mistakes in history have followed consciously reasoned decisions. If we're right 51 percent of the time in our impulsive actions we aren't doing badly.

The mistakes of inaction, flanked by heavy reasoning, are likely to be worse than the mistakes of genuine impulse. For one thing, they make our inertia worse day by day. Not long ago a woman whose husband had left her came to seek my advice. The difficulty between them appeared to be one of temperament which could be easily adjusted. And the woman told me that what she really wanted to do was simply to call her husband up and talk with him. I told her to follow that inclination. She left me somewhat at peace. But she didn't make the call; and in a few days she was back again. Once more she left with that impulse to call her husband. Unhappily, she never did. And a domestic rift that a few impulsive words on the phone might have healed finally ended in Reno. From childhood she had made time after time the mistake of letting her impulses die aborning.

We all know people who go through agonies of indecision before taking any important step. There are always arguments for and against, and the more we think about them the more they seem to offset each other, until we wind up in a state of paralysis. Impulsive action, which originates in a swift subconscious appraisal of the situation, might have saved all worry. And when a painfully thought-out decision proves wrong, how often we remember an original hunch that would have been right!

The way to get things done is to bring mind and muscle and voice into play at the very second a good impulse starts within us. I know a writer who was once engaged on a major project and was resolved that nothing could divert him from it. But he saw an announcement of a contest for the ten best rules for safe driving. The announcement flashes a light on the panel of his mind. Here was something he knew about. He interrupted his job long enough to get to a library and study up. He wrote 250 words. He turned in his entry in his own typing, not wanting to stop his stenographer from the bigger job. Months later that obeyed impulse netted him an award of $25,000. The project from which he turned aside for a moment brought him $600.

Or consider the young college instructor who sat listening one day to a commencement address by Woodrow Wilson, then governor of New Jersey. The instructor had written a book on political science, but had sought a publisher in vain. It embodied his innermost convictions and its apparent failure had caused him to despair of the future of his teaching.

Something Mr. Wilson said made the instructor feel that he ought to seek the governor's advice. He had heard that Wilson was cold and hard to approach; but at the end of the address he let his impulse carry him forward through the crowd; he grasped Mr. Wilson's hand, and said rapidly, "Your speech was wonderful! I've written a book maintaining that . . ." In a few pithy sentences he stated his theory.

Wilson shook his head. "No," he said. "You're wrong. I'll tell you why. See me after lunch at the Faculty Club." There for two hours Wilson talked earnestly. And under the inspiration Wilson gave him, the instructor wrote a new book. It sold more than 100,000 copies and launched him on a distinguished educational career. The first vital impulse, half-hesitantly obeyed, was the starting point.

The life stories of successful people are chock-full of episodes that have marked turning points in their careers. True impulses are intelligent. They reveal the basic interests of the unconscious mind.

There is in all of us an unceasing urge toward self-fulfillment. We know the kind of person we want to be because our impulses, even when enfeebled by disuse, tell us. Impulsive action is not to be substituted for reason but used as a means of showing the direction reason is to take. Obviously the path is not without pitfalls. To start suddenly throwing ourselves around on impulse might be hazardous. But at least we can begin responding oftener to inner urges that we know we can trust.

We *know* that in the midst of reading we ought to stop and look up a word if the meaning is not clear. We know that we ought to speak more words of unpremeditated praise where they are due. We know that we ought to wriggle out of selfish routine and take part in civic activities, that we ought to contribute not merely money but time to the well-being of the neighborhood.

Such separate moments of achievement are cumulative and result in enriched living, a consciousness of daily adventure, a long-term sense that life is not blocked out and cut-and-dried but may be managed from within. The man whose philosophy is summed up in the feeble and indecisive motto, "Well, we'll see about it," misses the savory moments of experience, the bounce and gusto of life.

Thumb back over the pages of your own experience and note how many of your happiest moments and greatest successes have followed spur-of-the-moment actions and decisions. They are reminders that only from the depths of your inner self can you hope for an invincible urge toward accomplishment. So, obey your best impulses and watch yourself go! 🕊

Hometown Hero: A Fine Bouquet

NANCY LAWLOR collects bouquets—flowers from hotels and weddings and corporate events, in cities like New York and Los Angeles. Then she gives them away to people in need, often breaking down larger bouquets so there's more to go around.

Lawlor was inspired to start her nonprofit organization, FlowerPower, in 2003.

Sitting in the lobby of the Waldorf Astoria, she was riveted by its towering floral displays. Where did they go at the end of the day? After getting her answer—a Dumpster—Lawlor volunteered to take them away instead. Once the hotel agreed, Lawlor delivered $2,000 worth of large pink bouquets to a New York City hospital. "It all started with one person saying yes," she says.

FlowerPower has distributed more than $2.5 million worth of flowers to hospitals, rape crisis centers, and rehabilitation clinics. The bouquets last several days, giving patients a healthy dose of good cheer. "I've seen thousands of people transformed," she says, "all over a simple bouquet of flowers that originally would've been thrown away." Now, that's a beautiful arrangement.

Natalie van der Meer

In Search of
Heaven

BY GAIL CAMERON WESCOTT

December 2005

I N AN unadorned room deep inside an Israeli maximum-security prison, a handsome Palestinian youth sits at a small wooden table across from television newscaster Barbara Walters. At age 17, the young man, who is now 21, attempted to set off a bomb on a crowded street to massacre as many people as possible, including himself. The bomb failed to go off. Now he will never leave this desolate place.

Walters, who is Jewish, wonders if he ever wanted a different life—to get married, have children, live normally.

"I thought about it," Jihad Jarrar answers matter-of-factly, "but I wanted to kill Jews." He believes his reward in the end will be to enter paradise—where he looks forward to joyous sex on silken couches amid rivers of milk and honey.

Walters's chilling encounter with the failed suicide bomber took place midway through a yearlong search for an answer to a question that has tantalized mankind from the beginning of time: What is heaven like, and who gets to go there? Even before beginning the project, a two-hour special called *Heaven* that aired on ABC, Walters had realized one indisputable fact: Most of us, regardless of our religious persuasion, do not think that life on earth ends here. We do not believe that this is all there is.

THERE ARE some 10,000 religions in the world, and nearly all incorporate teachings of an afterlife. In America, nine out of ten people believe that heaven is a real place—and most have faith that they are going there at the end of their lives.

Ask many of the faithful's children to describe heaven, and you will likely hear of angels perched on puffy clouds playing golden harps. But Walters does not remember ever thinking about heaven. Growing up in Boston and New York, the daughter of an impresario who launched the famous Latin Quarter nightclubs, she was raised in a secular world. "I didn't go to temple, and I didn't go to Sunday school," she says, "partly because my older sister was retarded and it would have been one more thing that Jackie could not do." Her family did not celebrate Yom Kippur—"the holiday that everybody we knew celebrated"—and at Christmas there were presents and stockings but never a tree.

While she unfailingly prays on planes, Walters spent little time devoted to spiritual matters as she carved out her iconic career. Dubbed "the alpha female of broadcast news," she spent 13 years on *The Today Show,* becoming its first female cohost. She then moved to ABC as the first woman coanchor of the network *Evening News,* commanding a then-unheard-of seven-figure salary. She spent 25 years at *20/20,* where she interviewed everyone from Presidents to Fidel Castro to Paris Hilton.

When Walters stepped down from the post, she agreed to produce specials for ABC. She set her sights first on the big story she had not done already: God and heaven. "It seemed the right time," she says. "There's so much interest in spirituality. Why are we here? Where are we going? We have e-mail and cell phones and the Internet, yet we see life whirling out of control."

For the special, Walters approached the subject with her signature candor. Sitting with Cardinal Theodore McCarrick, Archbishop of Washington, D.C., in the ornate cathedral of the National Shrine of the Immaculate Conception, she asked, "Is there sex in heaven?" He barely blinked. "That was a question they asked the Lord, and the answer was no."

In New York's famed Abyssinian Baptist Church, Rev. Calvin Butts, who has had multiple visions of heaven, revealed that his grandmother had spoken to him during her own funeral. "What did [she say]?" Walters asked. The grandmother explained why she once gave Butts's chicken and dumplings to the town drunk. "By doing good works, she was sending up a little timber for her heavenly home."

Whatever our vision, most of us expect heaven to be a better place. Evangelist Billy Graham has said he can't wait to get there. "I look forward to the reunion with friends and loved ones who have gone on before. I look forward to heaven's freedom from sorrow and pain."

Some, like Anthony DeStefano, author of *A Travel Guide to Heaven,* believe that in the afterlife we'll be able to go fishing with Hemingway, study piano with Mozart and painting with Michelangelo. Provided, he adds, that those folks make it to heaven.

To be sure, there is sometimes ruthless—even bloody—disagreement on exactly who gets in. When Walters asked the suicide bomber in Israel if she, as a non-Muslim, would be welcomed into paradise, his answer was swift and blunt: "No," he said. "Of course, you are going to hell."

On another day, in Colorado, Walters sat down with Ted Haggard, president of the National Association of Evangelicals. They are the most vocal force in U.S. religion today, with 40 million members. Walters asked if a person who did not accept Jesus Christ as his Savior was destined to go to hell. Haggard's answer was equally unambiguous: "Yes."

The interviewer herself, who purposely did not argue with her subjects, allowed afterward: "There are so many ways of looking at life and death. You just cannot say this belief is right and that is wrong. I think one of the major problems today is people saying that only my religion is right, and if you don't agree with me, you are not going to heaven."

At least for now, that view is not predominant in the United States. According to a recent Newsweek/Beliefnet poll, 79 percent of Americans believe that someone of another faith can attain salvation and go to heaven. But views of what heaven is vary widely among religious groups.

The world's 2.1 billion Christians believe that the purpose of life on earth is to get to heaven, a place of unending peace and tranquility where all tears and mourning cease. They believe that in heaven there will be an actual resurrection of the body. "We will look as we would want to look," says Cardinal McCarrick. Christians fully expect to see the people they loved on earth who preceded them. There will be no need for earthly pleasures there. Joy will come from being at one with God, roaming the universe in another dimension.

Muslims have a different, but equally rapturous, vision of heaven. In the Koran, paradise is described as a place where there will be lavishly comfortable homes with beautiful gardens and servants to attend to Islam's followers. (There are currently 1.2 billion of them.) Food and wine will be plentiful, and sex will be enjoyed by both men and women. Other Islamic texts promise that martyrs will be among the righteous Muslims who will be rewarded by sex with 72 virgins, a misunderstood concept, according to an Islamic scholar. The number was never meant to be a precise figure, he says, but an indication of "a surfeit of this kind of delight."

But not all religions have such a specific view of heaven. For most Jews, the idea of an afterlife is less important than what you do on earth. Still, almost all of the 14 million Jews in the world believe that there is life beyond death, when the body and soul separate and the soul goes off to be with God. The resurrection of the dead will occur at a time when the Messiah initiates a perfect world.

Buddhism doesn't teach that heaven is the soul's final resting place. Instead, the world's 350 million Buddhists believe in different heavens that lead you not to God but to nirvana, a place of enlightenment. Buddhists are born again and again, living many different lifetimes. Their behavior on earth determines the quality of their next life, and whether they return as a lowly animal or a person. Tibetan Buddhists believe that the Dalai Lama is godlike, the 14th reincarnation of a semidivine being.

To meet him, Walters traveled across the world to the village of Dharmshala, on the edge of the Himalayas in northern India, where the Dalai Lama settled when the Chinese took over his homeland more than four decades ago. "It was raining, and I was chilled to the bone for four days," says Walters, "but I was deeply affected by the Dalai Lama." Charming and charismatic, with a childlike giggle, he assured her he was not a god. Gods, he pointed out, did not get eye infections like the one afflicting him that day. "He said the purpose of life is to be happy," Walters remembers, "and the way to happiness is through compassion and warm-heartedness." In a world where wars are fought over religion, it struck her as a stunning concept. "For days afterward," says Walters, "I didn't have an angry thought or a competitive bone."

After her interview, Walters was moved to do something she never does. "I asked if I could give him a kiss on the cheek," she admits. He cheerfully agreed. Then he said he wanted to show her how it was done in New Zealand. In a misty rain in a distant corner of the world, the Dalai Lama and Barbara Walters rubbed noses.

By the conclusion of her journey, Walters had

talked not only with religious leaders but with people whose near-death experience had convinced them that they'd had an actual glimpse of heaven. She also met with Ellen Johnson, president of American Atheists, who believes that religion is superstition. "Heaven does not exist," Johnson says firmly. "Hell doesn't exist." She sees her acceptance of that fact as a means to make her life on earth more fulfilling because it is the only chance she'll have.

"I was deeply impressed by the sincerity of everyone I met," says Walters, sitting in her corner office at ABC, where a shelf is lined with Emmys. The newswoman declines to offer her own take on whether heaven exists. "I may not be certain what heaven is," she says, "but I do have a personal vision of hell. It's finishing a program and having someone come up to me after to say that I forgot to ask the most important question! And the person is usually right."

In the case of heaven, however, there will always be questions that cannot be answered—or even asked. "That's where faith comes in," Walters says. "Talking about heaven is talking about the meaning of life."

Quotable Quote

MY FATHER said there were two kinds of people in the world: givers and takers. The takers may eat better, but the givers sleep better. *Marlo Thomas*

Gilligan's Aisle

BY JEANNE MARIE LASKAS

December 1996

FROM *Washington Post Magazine*

HAVING BRAVED a Chicago snowstorm and rush-hour traffic, I trudged through O'Hare International Airport dragging my suitcase like a kid with a sled. There were people, bags, packages, babies, sour faces and airline representatives motioning like crossing guards. A monitor above our heads said "delayed" a few times and "canceled" a lot.

Three hours. That's how long my flight to Pittsburgh was delayed. *Three hours.*

I had two choices: I could lie to myself and say this

was a great opportunity to catch up on paperwork. Or I could plunge headfirst into a bad mood.

My gate was tucked away off the main corridor, a little peninsula unto itself. The only seats were next to other people, and I was in no mood for other people. *Who needs holidays anyway? And who needs snow?* I sat on the floor, folded my arms across my chest and adopted a look of quiet rage.

After about 20 minutes of examining every carpet stain within view, I looked up to see a lady with a Crate & Barrel shopping bag take a seat next to another lady with a Crate & Barrel shopping bag.

The first one introduced herself, opened her bag and rooted through tissue paper. "Twenty-five percent off!" she said, producing a bowl.

"Thirty-three percent off!" said the other, digging out a plate.

They laughed and started chattering away. The sound of such facile friendship was deeply annoying.

A businessman who was sitting behind them twisted in his seat and said something. The ladies cracked up.

A man with a cane seated one spot away joined in. Soon a purple-haired kid pulled off his earphones and started listening in. This happy group had a regular conversation going.

Must be nice, I allowed. *If you like that sort of thing.*

After an hour my lower back hurt. I got up and took the seat next to the kid. "And my mom and my dad split when I was four," he was telling the ladies.

"Aw," said one.

"Uh-huh," said the other.

The businessman caught my eye and said, "Don't I know you from somewhere?" We compared travel notes and found no intersections. He introduced me around anyway, and just like that I was in. We swapped stories: Forgotten luggage. Epic delays. Missed connections. Airport chair design.

A Gilligan's Island effect was taking place: we were stranded and having a great time.

A dark-haired man over by the window started snoring loudly. The businessman laughed, which we took as permission. We all broke up.

It was two hours more before a plane arrived at our gate. "What's the protocol here?" the businessman asked. "Should we applaud?" We took a vote: yes. So when the door opened and the people came out looking as miserable as each of us had felt, we stood up and clapped. The people were not amused.

"Hey, what book are you reading?" one of the Crate & Barrel ladies said to a stern-looking man carrying a novel. He stopped and stared. "Here," he said, handing over the book. "I'm done." Other passengers gave us magazines and newspapers.

When it came time to board, we lagged behind

our fellow travelers. The purple-haired kid carried the Crate & Barrel ladies' bags.

We were quiet now. We didn't know what to say. One of the ladies broke the silence: "Do you think we should have a reunion sometime?"

Laughter, the Best Medicine

PSYCHIATRY STUDENTS were in their Emotional Extremes class. "Let's set some parameters," the professor said. "What's the opposite of joy?" he asked one student. "Sadness," he answered. "The opposite of depression?" he asked another student. "Elation," he replied. "The opposite of woe?" the prof asked a young woman from Texas. The Texan replied, "Sir, I believe that would be giddyup."

• • •

I BOUGHT a pair of in-line skates, and a friend recommended I break them in by wearing them around the house. I practiced gliding over our carpet, leaving a number of indentations. Then I put the skates away.

When my husband came home, he exclaimed, "Vacuum-cleaner marks!" Giving me a big hug, he thanked me profusely for taking care of what is usually his weekend chore.   *Nancy Orr*

Miracles
Miracle
Miracles
Miracles
Miracles

The Gold-and-Ivory Tablecloth

BY REV. HOWARD C. SCHADE

December 1954

AT CHRISTMAS time men and women every-where gather in their churches to wonder anew at the greatest miracle the world has ever known. But the story I like best to recall was not a miracle—not exactly.

It happened to a pastor who was very young. His church was very old. Once, long ago, it had flourished. Famous men had preached from its pulpit, prayed before its altar. Rich and poor alike had worshiped there and built it beautifully. Now the good days had passed from the section of town where it stood. But the pastor and his young wife believed in their run-down church. They felt that with paint, hammer and faith they could get it in shape. Together they went to work.

But late in December a severe storm whipped through the river valley, and the worst blow fell on the little church—a huge chunk of rain-soaked plaster fell out of the inside wall just behind the altar. Sorrowfully the pastor and his wife swept away the mess, but they couldn't hide the ragged hole.

The pastor looked at it and had to remind himself quickly, "Thy will be done!" But his wife wept, "Christmas is only two days away!"

That afternoon the dispirited couple attended an auction held for the benefit of a youth group. The auctioneer opened a box and shook out of its folds a handsome gold-and-ivory lace tablecloth. It was a magnificent item, nearly 15 feet long. But it, too, dated from a long-vanished era. Who, today, had any use for such a thing? There were a few halfhearted bids. Then the pastor was seized with what he thought was a great idea. He bid it in for six dollars and fifty cents.

He carried the cloth back to the church and tacked it up on the wall behind the altar. It completely hid the hole! And the extraordinary beauty of its shimmering handwork cast a fine, holiday glow over the chancel. It was a great triumph. Happily he went back to preparing his Christmas sermon.

Just before noon on the day of Christmas Eve, as the pastor was opening the church, he noticed a woman standing in the cold at the bus stop.

"The bus won't be here for 40 minutes!" he called, and he invited her into the church to get warm.

She told him that she had come from the city that morning to be interviewed for a job as governess to the children of one of the wealthy families in town but she had been turned down. A war refugee, her English was imperfect.

The woman sat down in a pew and chafed her hands and rested. After a while she dropped her head and prayed. She looked up as the pastor began to adjust the great gold-and-ivory lace cloth across the hole. She rose suddenly and walked up the steps of the chancel. She looked at the tablecloth. The pastor smiled and started to tell her about the storm damage, but she didn't seem to listen. She took up a fold of the cloth and rubbed it between her fingers.

"It is mine!" she said. "It is my banquet cloth!" She lifted up a corner and showed the surprised pastor that there were initials monogrammed on it. "My husband had the cloth made especially for me in Brussels! There could not be another like it!"

For the next few minutes the woman and the pastor talked excitedly together. She explained that she was Viennese; that she and her husband had opposed the Nazis and decided to leave the country. They were advised to go separately. Her husband put her on a train for Switzerland. They planned that he would join her as soon as he could arrange to ship their household goods across the border.

She never saw him again. Later she heard that he had died in a concentration camp.

"I have always felt that it was my fault—to leave without him," she said. "Perhaps these years of wandering have been my punishment!"

The pastor tried to comfort her, urged her to take the cloth with her. She refused. Then she went away.

As the church began to fill on Christmas Eve, it was clear that the cloth was going to be a great success. It had been skillfully designed to look its best by candlelight.

After the service, the pastor stood at the doorway; many people told him that the church looked beautiful. One gentle-faced, middle-aged man—he was the local clock-and-watch repairman—looked rather puzzled.

"It is strange," he said in his soft accent. "Many years ago my wife—God rest her—and I owned such a cloth. In our home in Vienna, my wife put it on the table"—and here he smiled—"only when the bishop came to dinner!"

The pastor suddenly became very excited. He told the jeweler about the woman who had been in church earlier in the day.

The startled jeweler clutched the pastor's arm. "Can it be? Does she live?"

Together the two got in touch with the family who had interviewed her. Then, in the pastor's car they started for the city. And as Christmas Day was born this man and his wife—who had been separated through so many saddened Yuletides—were reunited.

To all who heard this story, the joyful purpose of the storm that had knocked a hole in the wall of the church was now quite clear. Of course people said it was a miracle, but I think you will agree it was the season for it! 🕊

Humor in the Face of Adversity

"SAY SOMETHING funny!" That's what people say when they find out I'm a comedian. But how would they feel if I found out they were a plumber and said, "Fix my sink!"? So when someone asks me to say something funny, I reply, "You're good-looking!" And they laugh. Usually.

Once at JFK airport, the customs guy looked at my paperwork and saw that I was a comedian. "Say something funny," he commanded.

"You're good-looking," I shot back.

There was a pause, followed by a smile. Then he pulled me aside and went through all my luggage.

Eddie Brill, for Reader's Digest

A Dog Like No Other

BY PETER MUILENBURG

June 1998

A WANING MOON had turned the muddy waters of Oyster Creek to quicksilver. Not so much as a zephyr stirred the inlet where our 42-foot ketch *Breath* lay in the delta of western Africa's mighty Gambia River near Banjul, the capital of Gambia. Days before, we'd sailed in off a thousand miles of ocean. Snug in this anchorage, we could still hear surf thundering just beyond the low span of the Denton Bridge.

The chance to see Africa had brought our family

back together for a couple of months. Our older son, Rafael, 20, had taken leave from college to join the rest of us: Diego, 13, my wife, Dorothy, and our little black dog, Santos.

Breath had been our only home since I had built the vessel on St. John in the Virgin Islands in the early 1980s. Life afloat had knit close bonds. Everyone had responsibilities—the boys were standing watch when they were six. And for the past eight years, Santos, our loving, feisty, 11-pound schipperke, was at our side.

When we went to bed that night, Santos lay on the cabin top, which he vacated only in the worst weather. He touched his nose to Dorothy's face as she bent low to nuzzle him good night. His ardent eyes flared briefly—he worshiped her—then he returned to his duty.

We slept easier with him aboard. It was his self-appointed mission to ensure that no one, friend or foe, approached within 100 yards of *Breath* without a warning. He'd sailed with us through the Caribbean, the Atlantic and the Mediterranean, keeping sharp watch and good company, and bringing us luck. In eight years we'd never suffered a mishap. But during the night of January 2, 1991, that would change.

We were asleep when, just past midnight, our dock lines began to creak. At first I thought a passing boat might have sent a wake, but Santos would have barked. The creaking grew louder. By the time I climbed on deck, the ropes groaned against the cleats that tethered our boat to another vessel.

On such a calm night there could be only one cause—current. My boat was tied stern to stream, and a glance over the side at water speeding past the hull alarmed me. The ebb had tripled its usual spring-tide rate. The cleats on the other boat looked ready to snap. If anything gave, both vessels could spin off bound together, helpless to avoid destruction. I had to cast off.

We were in a difficult spot. Just a few boat-lengths downstream, two high-tension power lines hung across the creek. About 100 feet behind them loomed Denton Bridge. If we couldn't turn in time, our metal mainmast might hit the wires. If the boat hit the bridge, both masts would be pinned by the roadway while the hull was sucked under.

I called everyone up on deck. Sensing something was wrong, Santos stood by, poised to react.

We cast off the lines and hung briefly to a stern anchor, but we had to let go as *Breath* was swung violently back and forth by the current's force. I gunned the engine and had almost turned the boat around when I realized that, dragged toward the bridge by the current, we were going to hit the power line. Dorothy clutched a quivering Santos, and we all held our breath.

We just tipped the wire. There was a meteor shower of sparks and we were through, but the second wire was coming up fast. I flung the wheel over hard, but we struck the wire anyway—a long, scraping skid, the top six inches of our mast pinned against the power line.

Electricity exploded down the rigging, and a hideous incandescence lit the sky. Flames leapt up inside the cabin; fuses shot from their sockets; smoke billowed out the hatches.

Then the fireworks stopped. The cable had rolled over the mast, but we were trapped between the second wire and the bridge. There was nowhere to go but back out—through the wire. Santos wriggled out of Dorothy's arms and dashed up to the foredeck to be in on the action.

The wheel hard over, we braced for impact. The mast top hit the cable, sending down a torrent of red sparks. Santos, eyes fixed ahead, stood his ground to defend the foredeck. He was growling for all he was worth when sparks landed in his fur. Uttering a high-pitched scream, he sprinted down the side deck, cinders glowing in his coat, and plunged into the water. When he surfaced, Santos was swimming for the boat, his eyes fastened on Dorothy. But the current swept him into the shadows under Denton Bridge and out of sight.

An instant later a blast like a small thunderbolt hit the mainstay. My son Raffy was flipped backward off the foredeck and into the water.

Then we were through. Diego seized a fire extinguisher and attacked the flames as I steered toward a trawler tied to a concrete slab on the muddy bank. Raffy, a college swimmer, managed to get to the bank.

Against all odds we were safe—except for Santos. Raffy called along both shores, but there was no sign of him. We spent the rest of the night tied to the trawler. As I tried to sleep, I kept thinking of Santos. I felt a helpless sorrow over his fate.

The next day Dorothy walked for miles down the beach, making inquiries at every hotel, talking to beach attendants, tourists, vendors. Nobody had seen our little black dog.

She offered a reward over the ship's radio, notified the police and nailed up signs. It was touching, but it seemed futile to me. Just beyond the bridge were broad flats of sand pounded that night by row after row of massive breakers. The thought of Santos funneled helplessly into the surf made me wince.

Days later we'd repaired *Breath*, but Santos still hadn't turned up. "Honey," I told Dorothy, "we've got to get on with our life—do the river, cross the Atlantic, get back to work."

"But what if he survived?" she asked. "What if he finds his way back, and we're gone?"

"It's hard to believe he survived that surf," I said flatly, "and then swam till dawn."

She searched my face, looking for a reprieve from

reality. Then her eyes flooded and her voice broke. "I just didn't want to abandon him."

With heavy hearts the next morning, we hauled the anchor for our trip upriver.

Our loss really hit home 50 miles upstream where we anchored. Suddenly a strange face peered in the porthole and inquired if we wanted to buy a fish. The fisherman had paddled up silently alongside. When Santos was alive, that could never have happened. Now we sorely missed the zealous barking we'd so often tried to hush.

Not a day went by without someone bringing up another Santos story. He might have been small, but he was absolutely fearless. Santos had a classic Napoleon complex. He had to have respect, and he got it by making bigger animals run from him. He was all bluff. But with a histrionically vicious growl and a headlong charge, he had put to flight Rottweilers, herds of goats, troops of wild donkeys, even a meter reader.

Once, on the island of St. Lucia, an elephant brought over by a rich estate owner emerged from the woods into a clearing where Santos was merrily scattering a flock of chickens. Our dog reacted in character: he charged. The elephant panicked, flaring its ears, splitting the air with its trumpet call and smacking the ground with its trunk as Santos dodged and darted underfoot. We had to catch Santos and drag him away.

We'd never see another like him, I thought as I steered upriver.

Soon after, I woke one night to an empty bed. I found Dorothy sitting in the moonlight. From the way her eyes glistened, I could tell she'd been thinking of Santos. I sat down and put an arm around her. After a while she spoke. "You know what I miss most? His shaggy mane filling the porthole. He liked to watch me cook. Now every time a shadow falls over that port, it reminds me of the love in those bright black eyes."

We watched the moon slip below the treetops; then, our hearts filled with grief, we went back to bed.

Two weeks passed as we made our way 150 miles up the Gambia River. One afternoon Dorothy and I were reinforcing the deck awning when I saw a catamaran with a man on board inspecting us with binoculars.

"Are you the Americans who lost the dog?" he called.

"Yes," I said cautiously.

"I don't know if it is yours, but the police at Denton Bridge have a small black dog found on the beach."

Everyone tumbled up on deck shouting, "Oh, my God! Yes! Yes!" But I cautioned, "Someone might have found a stray mutt and brought it in, hoping for the reward. Don't get your hopes too high."

Dorothy and I took a series of bush taxis and old

buses back to Banjul the next morning. With hope and trepidation we caught a taxi to Denton Bridge to see if Santos had truly survived.

"You've come for your dog!" the police officer on duty greeted us. He turned and called to a boy, "Go bring the dog." Dorothy and I waited on tenterhooks.

Then, led on a ratty piece of string down the path, there was Santos. He walked with a limp, head down. But when Dorothy called "Santos," his head shot up, his ears snapped forward, his whole body trembled as that beloved voice registered. He leapt into her arms and covered her face with licks. Dorothy hugged him, her eyes filled with tears.

The police officer told us that the morning after we'd hit the power lines, a Swedish tourist was walking the beach and found Santos—six miles from Oyster Creek. The Swede smuggled the wet, hungry animal into his hotel room and fed him. When the Swede had to fly home, he gave Santos to the police.

We noticed Santos's muzzle seemed whiter, and when we patted him on his right flank, he sometimes yelped in pain. We wondered what he'd experienced as he was swept into the surf and carried along the coast. We marveled at his fortitude and his luck. But most of all we were grateful to have him back.

Next morning we made our way back upriver. We arrived just after sundown and shouted for the boys.

"Do you have him?" they called. Dorothy urged the

dog to bark. His unmistakable voice rang across the river, to be answered by a cheer of wild exuberance.

Later that night we toasted Santos with lemonade. No need for champagne when euphoria spiced the air we breathed. Santos was back. Our family was intact. 🕊

Life in These United States

MY WIFE and I were looking at paintings in a gallery. One was of a beautiful nude woman with only a little foliage covering her private areas.

"Bad taste," muttered my wife, and moved on. Not me. I lingered, completely transfixed, until I heard her shout, "What are you waiting for—autumn?" *Dennis Dook*

• • •

ROBBIE, MY nine-year-old grandson, recently asked his mother about puberty. She explained that it occurs when children's bodies begin to change. "Boys," she said, "grow taller and develop muscles. Their voices deepen, and they start to grow hair, like facial hair." She paused. "Do you understand?"

"Yes," he replied. "I just hope it happens on a Saturday, when I'm not in school." *Michael Stephenson*

"A Man Don't Know What He Can Do"

BY ELISE MILLER DAVIS

October 1952

JUST BEFORE midnight Roy Gaby, driving for a Houston, Texas, trucking company, ran out of gasoline while returning from Waco in a heavy 14-wheel truck-trailer. From a house nearby he telephoned his wife, "SOS, honey, I'm out of gas." Mrs. Gaby sighed, bundled up the baby and set out to the rescue in the family car. It was February 18, 1952.

On the way home Mrs. Gaby drove ahead of Roy. About ten miles from Houston a speeding car, with an apparently drunken driver who never stopped, darted out of a side road, forcing Mrs. Gaby's car off the highway on the right. In the rearview mirror she caught a glimpse of Roy's truck swerving to avoid a collision. Then she heard a crash.

The engine had smashed into a mammoth oak tree, the trailer had piled up on the cab and Roy was trapped in the twisted debris.

A passing motorist rushed into the village of Fairbanks and notified Deputy Sheriff Don Henry.

Henry decided to try "untelescoping" the wreck. "We attached a wrecker to the front of the mashed-in engine, hoping to pull it straight enough to get Gaby out. But the idea didn't work. We added the power of a truck at the front of the wrecker. Finally two more trucks were attached to the rear, and they pulled in the opposite direction. But still, no soap."

Small flames appeared beneath the truck, and there was no extinguisher at hand. Halting passing drivers, Henry set helpers to working frantically at the crumpled doors with hammers and crowbars. The twisted doors refused to budge. Henry crawled onto the hood of the cab and turned his flashlight on the victim. The steering wheel was crushed against Gaby's waist and his feet were pinned between twisted brake and clutch pedals. Tiny flames were licking at his feet.

"I'm an accident investigator," Henry told me later, "and I've seen a lot of terrible sights. But I've never seen one more terrible and I've never felt more helpless. I looked at Mrs. Gaby and the baby, then back at the poor guy in the burning cab, and I felt like praying for a miracle."

At that moment, a husky black man appeared out of the darkness.

"Can I help?" he asked quietly. Henry shook his head. Nobody could help if three trucks and a wrecker couldn't budge that cab, and by the time cutting torchers and fire apparatus arrived it was going to be just too bad. The stranger calmly walked over to the cab, put his hands on the door and *wrenched it off!*

Speechless, the crowd watched him reach in the cab and tear out the burning floor mat. Then he put out the flames around Gaby's legs—with his bare hands.

"It was just about then that I caught a glimpse of the big fellow's face," said one of the witnesses. "At first I thought he was in a trance. Then I saw that set expression for what it was—cold, calculated fury. I'd seen it before—at Pearl Harbor, on Okinawa. I remember thinking: *Why, that guy's not calm, he's enraged.* It was just as if he despised fire."

Swiftly, almost as if rehearsed, the black man worked on, poking large arms into the truck cab. "He straightened that steering wheel like it was tin," the driver of the wrecker said. "With his left hand on the brake pedal and his right on the clutch, he all but uprooted the whole works to free Gaby's feet."

But the crucial job wasn't done. The victim still lay encased in what witnesses called "a squashed sardine can over a bonfire."

Patiently, then stubbornly, the big man struggled to squeeze in beside Gaby. The space was too tiny. Stepping back from the cab, he hesitated fleetingly. The flames were growing. He glared at them, slumped to a squatting position and began pushing into the cab, fighting crazily. At long last he was in far enough to rest his feet firmly on the floorboard. He started rising slowly. His muscles bulged in the half-light and the sleeves of his shirt tore.

"My God, he's trying to push up the top!" a woman's voice called.

Neck and shoulders against the caved-in cab roof, he pushed. Hard.

"We actually heard the metal give," reported a farmer who had come to the scene. Discussing the rescue afterward, Deputy Henry shook his head, still baffled. "And he held that top up until we could pull Gaby out."

In the excitement of attending Gaby, no one thought to thank the stranger or even ask his name. Later, at the hospital with Gaby, Deputy Henry told newsmen: "The mysterious Samson disappeared as quietly as he'd come. If I hadn't witnessed it I'd never believe a lone man could do a job we couldn't do with three trucks and a wrecker."

"I wish I knew his name," put in Mrs. Gaby. "He was a giant."

No giant, 33-year-old Charles Dennis Jones was in fact six-feet-two inches tall and weighed 220 pounds. He'd been out to nearby Hempstead to change tires on a disabled truck when he came upon the accident. By morning the whole city of Houston was wondering about his identity. Newspapers throughout the country carried the story. But Jones didn't tell even his wife about his experience. His boss, C. C. Myers, became suspicious, however, when he noticed the big fellow walk away from a group of employees who were discussing the amazing rescue. Remembering the mission he'd sent Jones on the night before, Myers grabbed a photograph from company files and headed for the sheriff's office. "Yes, that's him," agreed Deputy Henry.

And Myers knew immediately how Charlie Jones found the strength to lick that fire.

ONE DECEMBER night 14 months before, Jones had come home to the three-room house where he lived with his wife, Mildred, and their five small children. Under one arm he carried a tiny pine tree and a single string of Christmas lights.

They'd had a lot of bad luck that year. Only two months before both his mother and Mildred's had died within a week, leaving grief, doctor bills, funeral expenses. But Evelyn Carol, his eight-year-old first-born, wanted some *real* Christmas-tree lights and he had them. He'd manage. He was healthy and husky and could stand a 16-hour day. Double work meant double pay. And they had a roof over their heads. Paid for.

Mildred left for church, where she was singing that evening. Jones tucked in the children. As he undressed, he wondered if he should risk leaving the tree lights on. He decided he would. Evelyn Carol wanted to surprise her mother and he'd promised. He fell asleep.

Mildred's pillow was still untouched when Jones awoke, sure he was having a nightmare. There was a burning in his nostrils, a crackling sound in his ears. He heard a child's cry: "Daddy!" Instantly he was on his feet, awake in a world on fire, pushing through choking waves of smoke, grabbing small bodies until he counted five, finding his way to the open window, pitching the children out.

People gathered. And Mildred came running through the darkness, crying his name. Then Jones heard a man's voice, maybe his own: "No, no—Evelyn Carol, come back, come back!" A child's answer: "But I must get my Christmas lights!" And like a fleeting spirit Evelyn Carol in a little white nightgown ran back toward the flames.

Later a neighbor told how the men couldn't hold Jones. How he'd raced after his child but hadn't reached her because just as he neared the dwelling its last remains exploded. How the blast had thrown Jones to the ground unconscious, and he'd been dragged out of danger.

The next morning, for the first time in ten years, Charles Dennis Jones failed to report to work at Robertson Transport. Everybody there had heard. When a man loses a child and his home, has four children to support and another one on the way, what can other men do?

Before nine o'clock a paper was circulating—from workshops to offices to yards. By noon it bore the names of 84 Robertson employees, and was sealed in an envelope and delivered to Charlie Jones. In the envelope Jones found $765.50.

The following day friends at Hughes Tool Company, where Mildred had formerly worked, sent in $80. By mail, from strangers, came $16. There were countless offers: Can you use a refrigerator? An army cot? A boy's coat, size six? It seemed everyone had united to help the Jones family. And before long Charlie began to work on a new home. He figured that before the new baby came he'd have his family back under their own roof.

You could understand why he always would hate fire.

Reading a newspaper account of Jones's heroic rescue, R. A. Childers, a Houston businessman, wrote the papers, saying he would give $400 to start a fund providing an annual college scholarship for a black high school graduate. The rescue had taken place during Brotherhood Week. "Could anything be more characteristic of brotherhood than the fact that Jones walked away without waiting for thanks?" Childers asked.

And so it came about in the new house Charlie and Mildred and their children had built with their own hands that they received a group of citizens who informed them of the proposed Charles D. Jones Endowment Fund. Jones heard the committee's proposal in his faded blue overalls, eyes glazed by unshed tears. His wife stood beside him, his children huddled near. He didn't say a word.

Finally, Childers broke the silence. Somehow Charlie must give a statement to the press. There was the mystery he might yet clear up. How in the name of heaven had he managed to wrench off a steel door, beat out flames with his hands, raise with his own back the crushed-in top of a driver's cab?

Charlie Jones looked at Childers and at the hushed group around him. He cleared his throat and said, simply:

"A man don't know what he can do until another man is hurting." 🦢

All Our Problems, Solved!

SCENE: A preschool class on plants.
    Teacher: This plant grows something red and round that we use to make spaghetti sauce. What is it?
    Student: Meatballs.
                                                        Donanne Seese

The Forked-Stick Phenomenon

BY EMILY AND PER OLA D'AULAIRE

May 1976

CONDENSED FROM *Saturday Evening Post*

D OWSING, AS a way of locating underground water, lacks any scientific basis, according to most geologists. How then, to account for its many successes?

A well-dressed man strolls across a meadow on his 130-acre Connecticut farm, a forked twig gripped between his upturned hands. Onlookers giggle. He ignores them, concentrating on the stick. Near a corner of the field, the tip of the twig suddenly turns down, seemingly pulled by some other-worldly force. He carefully marks the spot, and then calls in a well driller, telling him there's water—plenty of it—about 125 feet down. The driller shrugs. "It's your money," he says, and starts work.

Later comes the call: "We've hit an underground river! At 127 feet. Enough water for the whole town."

That is what happened to Joseph Baum, a Hartford, Connecticut, advertising executive, ten years ago when he needed water for his farm. Baum had been skeptical about dowsing, but changed his mind back in 1950 after reluctantly joining a friend on a dowsing expedition. Soon, people were calling him a dowser, a diviner, a water witch. Since that time he has located some two dozen wells for other people, and even written a book on the subject.*

This kind of innate ability to find water has fascinated mankind for centuries. Sir Isaac Newton is said to have tried dowsing, and been intrigued. Reputedly, Thomas Edison attributed successful dowsing to electricity—while Albert Einstein thought the explanation lay in electromagnetism. The American Society of Dowsers estimates that nearly a quarter-million water wells sunk on the Atlantic seaboard since Colonial times have been located by "witching." Today, some 25,000 people like Baum practice the arcane art in the United States, while millions more may possess the skill.

*The Beginner's Handbook of Dowsing, Crown.

One of those maddeningly slippery phenomena that slide back and forth between truth and fiction, dowsing has long been a subject of controversy. Skeptics scoff at it as illogical, ridiculous, scientifically impossible. (Dowsers, in turn, point out that aerodynamically, bumblebees can't fly.) Geologists claim that in many places water can be found no matter where one digs. Then why, counter the dowsers, can they often find water where trained geologists can't?

Take the case of New Sharon, Maine, a small town which until last summer was so short of water that residents were restricted to one bath a week. In five years, the town had sunk $180,000 worth of federal loans into geological studies and deep wells that consistently turned up dry. As a last resort, community officials hired a professional dowser for $500. Armed with his divining rod, he shortly located a site. When drilled, the well provided all the water the town could use.

Or take the case of the Shoreline Clinic in Essex, Connecticut. This million-dollar regional health-care center was nearing completion in 1975. Though several thousand dollars had been spent, engineers found themselves unable to get sufficient water from four wells sunk at sites deemed hydrologically most promising. A local water witch volunteered his services. Following the pull of his V-shaped fiberglass divining rod, he headed toward the rear of the clinic property. There the stick suddenly bobbed earthward. A drill rig started work, and soon there was a new well, yielding 20 gallons a minute—plenty of water for the new clinic.

"Just because science can't explain it doesn't mean dowsing can't work," says Baum. "We are still surrounded by mysteries here on earth which at present cannot be explained."

The practice of dowsing goes back for millennia. Archeologists found an 8,000-year-old cave painting in North Africa's Atlas Mountains which shows a dowser, divining rod in hand, surrounded by a group of onlookers. The idea of the magic wand may well have begun with the divining rod. Some scholars trace the work of dowsers through Biblical times. When Moses smote the rock to bring forth water in the wilderness, was he in fact dowsing?

Although the forked stick has become the classic instrument for dowsing, a wide variety of tools have been used over the ages: whalebone, crowbars, pliers, blades of grass, even bare hands. Today, plastic, metal or fiberglass V-rods are favored by some dowsers, since they are smoother than a tree branch to hold. (The forked stick is reported to react so violently at times that the dowser's hands are left red and raw, and the bark peels off the twig.) The ability, however, lies not in the tool but in the user. Whether the dowser is aware of it or not, it is he or she who moves the rod.

Dowsing is used for more than discovering water wells. Plumbers have long used "pipe locaters"—twin L-shaped dowsing rods made of bent wire that seem to swing apart or together when over buried water lines. Some utility companies employ dowsers to zero in on telephone cables, water mains, and electrical power lines prior to digging. In Vietnam, engineer units of the 1st and 3rd Marine divisions successfully used bent coat hangers to locate enemy tunnels, booby traps and mines.

Soviet scientists are actively using dowsing, which they call the Biophysical Method (BPM), to detect ore bodies, subterranean streams and oil. At a 1973 conference in Prague, Soviet professor Aleksandr Bakirov reported that BPM has proved of definite value in geological mapping—in establishing fissured zones and geological contact zones, in tracing mineralized zones. "It makes prospecting more effective and also lowers the cost of drilling," he says.

Is there a physiological basis for the skill? In the United States, physicist Zaboj V. Harvalik has found that many dowsers are unconsciously sensitive to small disturbances in the earth's magnetic field. In tests, he has had subjects walk across a low-intensity electromagnetic beam that can be switched on and off. Sensitive dowsers seem to pick up "dowsing signals" from it. Yet they fail to do so when certain parts of their bodies—the kidney area, or the head—are shielded with heavy aluminum or copper foil. This suggests the existence of magnetic sensors in those parts of the body, as well as a "signal processor" in the brain which transmits the command for subliminal arm-muscle contractions that move the rod. Says Harvalik: "The rod turns not because it is pulled by some unknown force, but because certain individuals sense a change deep in the earth."

Some further explanation is needed, however, to account for "long-distance" or "map" dowsing. In one of the most famous cases on record, documented by American historical novelist Kenneth Roberts in 1950, dowser Henry Gross spread out a map of Bermuda in Roberts's home in Kennebunkport, Maine. Then, passing his divining rod over it, he marked three places in Bermuda where fresh water was to be found—despite geologists' conviction that no fresh water existed on the island. The Bermuda government was persuaded to provide drilling equipment, and by April 1950 all three wells had come in. One of them alone was providing a total of 63,360 gallons daily.

"Dowsing is a parapsychological phenomenon—ESP," says Karlis Osis, of the American Society for Psychical Research. It works, he says, because humans unconsciously know a broad spectrum of things that lie beyond the range of normal awareness—perhaps through the 75 percent of brainpower seemingly unused in everyday life. Some of this information, hidden deep in the mind, may indirectly filter into consciousness through slight physiological changes demonstrated by muscular movements and an indicator such as a divining rod.

The American Society of Dowsers, which is composed of 1,400 true believers from all walks of life—teachers, farmers, doctors, housewives—convenes each September at its headquarters in Danville, Vermont. There last fall, as a test, we asked Maine dowser Bob Ater if he could locate the well on our property in Connecticut, over 300 miles away. He told us to draw a rough map of the property, including any buildings. Shown our finished sketch, he asked, "What about the old foundation over there?" For a moment, we thought he had to be mistaken—but then we remembered an overgrown concrete slab, where a garage had stood 30 years ago. We traced it in.

Ater picked up a pencil, which he explained acted as a dowsing rod for him. He poised it over the map. Then his hand descended, and he marked a neat little circle—just about where our well is.

As an afterthought, he said, "There seems to be something coming out of the house over here." He drew a snakelike line from the end of our house, along the driveway, to the terrace. We stared in disbelief. It was where we had left the garden hose—and exactly where we found it when we returned home two days later. 🪶

Letter in the Wallet

BY ARNOLD FINE

September 1985

FROM *The Jewish Press*

I T WAS a freezing day, a few years ago, when I stumbled on a wallet in the street. There was no identification inside. Just three dollars and a crumpled letter that looked as if it had been carried around for years.

The only thing legible on the torn envelope was the return address. I opened the letter and saw that it had been written in 1924—almost 60 years ago. I read it carefully, hoping to find some clue to the identity of the wallet's owner.

It was a "Dear John" letter. The writer, in a delicate

script, told the recipient, whose name was Michael, that her mother forbade her to see him again. Nevertheless, she would always love him. It was signed, Hannah.

It was a beautiful letter. But there was no way, beyond the name Michael, to identify the owner. So I called information to see if the operator could help.

"Operator, this is an unusual request. I'm trying to find the owner of a wallet I found. Is there any way you could tell me the phone number for an address that was on a letter in the wallet?"

The operator gave me her supervisor, who said there was a phone listed at the address but that she could not give me that number. However, she would call and explain the situation. Then, if the party wanted to talk, she would connect me. I waited a minute, and she came back on the line. "I have a woman who will speak with you."

I asked the woman if she knew a Hannah.

"Oh, of course! We bought this house from Hannah's family."

"Would you know where they could be located now?" I asked.

"Hannah had to place her mother in a nursing home years ago. Maybe the home could help you track down the daughter."

The woman gave me the name of the nursing home. I called and found out that Hannah's mother had died. The woman I spoke with gave me an address where she thought Hannah could be reached.

I phoned. The woman who answered explained that Hannah herself was now living in a nursing home. She gave me the number. I called and was told, "Yes, Hannah is with us."

I asked if I could stop by to see her. It was almost 10:00 p.m. The director said that Hannah might be asleep. "But if you want to take a chance, maybe she's in the dayroom watching television."

The director and a guard greeted me at the door of the nursing home. We went up to the third floor and saw the nurse, who told us that Hannah was indeed watching TV.

We entered the dayroom. Hannah was a sweet, silver-haired old-timer with a warm smile and friendly eyes. I told her about the wallet and showed her the letter. The second she saw it, she took a deep breath. "Young man," she said, "this letter was the last contact I had with Michael." She looked away, then said pensively, "I loved him very much. But I was only 16, and my mother felt I was too young. He was so handsome. You know, like Sean Connery, the actor."

We both laughed. The director then left us alone. "Yes, Michael Goldstein was his name. If you find him, tell him I still think of him often. I never did marry," she said, smiling through tears that welled up in her eyes. "I guess no one ever matched up to Michael. . . ."

I thanked Hannah, said good-bye, and took the

elevator to the first floor. As I stood at the door, the guard asked, "Was she able to help you?"

I told him she had given me a lead. "At least I have a last name. But I probably won't pursue it further for a while." I explained that I had spent almost the whole day trying to find the wallet's owner.

While we talked, I pulled out the brown-leather case with its red-lanyard lacing and showed it to the guard. He looked at it and said, "Hey, I'd know that anywhere. That's Mr. Goldstein's. He's always losing it. I found it in the hall at least three times."

"Who's Mr. Goldstein?" I asked.

"He's one of the old-timers on the eighth floor. That's Mike Goldstein's wallet, for sure. He goes out for a walk quite often."

I thanked the guard and ran back to the director's office to tell him what the guard had said. He accompanied me to the eighth floor. I prayed that Mr. Goldstein would be up.

"I think he's still in the dayroom," the nurse said. "He likes to read at night. . . . A darling man."

We went to the only room that had lights on, and there was a man reading a book. The director asked him if he had lost his wallet.

Michael Goldstein looked up, felt his back pocket, and then said, "Goodness, it *is* missing."

"This kind gentleman found a wallet. Could it be yours?"

The second he saw it, he smiled with relief. "Yes," he said, "that's it. Must have dropped it this afternoon. I want to give you a reward."

"Oh, no thank you," I said. "But I have to tell you something. I read the letter in the hope of finding out who owned the wallet."

The smile on his face disappeared. "You read that letter?"

"Not only did I read it, I think I know where Hannah is."

He grew pale. "Hannah? You know where she is? How is she? Is she still as pretty as she was?"

I hesitated.

"Please tell me!" Michael urged.

"She's fine, and just as pretty as when you knew her."

"Could you tell me where she is? I want to call her tomorrow." He grabbed my hand and said, "You know something? When that letter came, my life ended. I never married. I guess I've always loved her."

"Michael," I said. "Come with me."

The three of us took the elevator to the third floor. We walked toward the dayroom where Hannah was sitting, still watching TV. The director went over to her.

"Hannah," he said softly. "Do you know this man?" Michael and I stood waiting in the doorway.

She adjusted her glasses, looked for a moment, but didn't say a word.

"Hannah, it's Michael. Michael Goldstein. Do you remember?"

"Michael? Michael? It's you!"

He walked slowly to her side. She stood, and they embraced. The two of them sat on a couch, held hands and started to talk. The director and I walked out, both of us crying.

"See how the good Lord works," I said philosophically. "If it's meant to be, it will be."

Three weeks later, I got a call from the director, who asked, "Can you break away on Sunday to attend a wedding?"

He didn't wait for an answer. "Yup, Michael and Hannah are going to tie the knot!"

It was a lovely wedding, with all the people at the nursing home joining in the celebration. Hannah wore a beige dress and looked beautiful. Michael wore a dark-blue suit and stood tall. The home gave them their own room, and if you ever wanted to see a 76-year-old bride and a 78-year-old groom acting like two teenagers, you had to see this couple.

A perfect ending for a love affair that had lasted nearly 60 years.

Gratitud
Gratitude
Gratitud
Gratitude
Gratitude

Christopher Reeve's Decision

BY **CHRISTOPHER REEVE**

July 1998

CONDENSED FROM *Still Me*

O N MEMORIAL Day weekend, 1995, my world changed forever. I was competing in an equestrian event in Virginia when my horse, Buck, decided to put on the brakes just before the third jump.

When he stopped suddenly, momentum carried me over the top of his head. My hands got entangled in the bridle, and I couldn't get an arm free to break my fall. All six-feet-four-inches and 215 pounds of me landed headfirst. Within seconds I was paralyzed from the neck down and fighting for air like a drowning person.

I woke up five days later in the intensive-care unit at the University of Virginia hospital. Dr. John Jane, head of neurosurgery at the hospital, said I had broken the top two cervical vertebrae and that I was extremely lucky to have survived. He told my wife, Dana, and me that I might never be able to breathe on my own again. But my head was intact, and my brain stem—so close to the site of the injury—appeared unharmed.

Dr. Jane said my skull would have to be reconnected to my spinal column. He wasn't sure if the operation would be successful, or even if I could survive.

Suddenly it dawned on me that I was going to be a huge burden to everybody, that I had ruined my life and everybody else's. *Why not die,* I thought miserably, *and save everyone a lot of trouble?*

As family and friends visited, my spirits were on a roller-coaster ride. I would feel so grateful when someone came a long way to cheer me up. But the time would come when everybody had to leave, and I'd lie there and stare at the wall, stare at the future, stare in disbelief.

When I would finally fall asleep, I'd be whole again, making love to Dana, riding or acting in a play. Then I'd wake up and realize that I could no longer do any of that; I was just taking up space.

One day Dana came into the room and stood beside me. I could not talk because of the ventilator. But as we made eye contact, I mouthed the words, "Maybe we should let me go."

Dana started crying. "I am only going to say this once," she said. "I will support whatever you want to do because this is your life and your decision. But I want you to know that I'll be with you for the long haul, no matter what."

Then she added the words that saved my life: "You're still you. And I love you."

I can't drift away from this, I began to realize. *I don't want to leave.*

A CRISIS like my accident doesn't change a marriage; it brings out what is truly there. It intensifies but does not transform it. Dana rescued me when I was lying in Virginia with a broken body, but that was really the second time. The first time was the night we met.

It was June 1987, and a long-term relationship of mine had ended. I was determined to be alone and focus on my work. Since childhood I had developed the belief that a few isolated moments of happiness were the best you could hope for in relationships. I didn't want to risk too much because I was certain that disappointment would follow.

Then one night I went to a cabaret with friends, and Dana Morosini stepped onstage. She wore an off-the-shoulder dress and sang "The Music That Makes Me Dance." I went down hook, line and sinker.

Afterward I went backstage and introduced myself. At the time, I was an established film actor. You wouldn't think I'd have a problem with a simple conversation with a woman. But when I offered her a ride to the party we were all going to, she said, "No thanks, I have my own car." All I could say was "Oh." I dragged myself out to my old pickup truck, trying to plan my next move.

Later I tried again. We talked for a solid hour. I have no idea what we talked about. Everything seemed to evaporate around us. I thought to myself, *I don't want to make a mistake and ruin this.*

We started dating in a very old-fashioned way. I got to know Dana's parents, and we developed an easy rapport. And Dana was instantly comfortable with my two children, Matthew and Alexandra. It filled me with joy.

Dana and I were married in April 1992. Three years later came my accident and Dana's words in the hospital room: "You're still you."

I mouthed, "This goes way beyond the marriage vows—'in sickness and in health.'" She said, "I know." I knew then and there that she was going to be with me forever. We had become a family.

AS THE operation drew closer, I became more frightened, knowing I had only a 50-50 chance of surviving. I lay frozen much of the time, thinking dark thoughts.

My biggest fear had to do with breathing. I couldn't

take a single breath on my own, and the ventilator connections didn't always hold. I would lie there at three in the morning in fear of a pop-off, when the hose just comes off the ventilator. After you've missed two breaths, an alarm sounds. You hope someone will come quickly. The feeling of helplessness was hard to take.

One very bleak day the door to my room flew open and in hurried a squat fellow in a surgical gown and glasses, speaking with a Russian accent. He said he was my proctologist and had to examine me immediately.

My first thought was that they must be giving me way too many drugs. But it was my old friend, comedian Robin Williams. For the first time since the accident, I laughed.

My three-year-old, Will, also gave me hope. One day he was on the floor playing when he suddenly looked up and said, "Mommy, Daddy can't move his arms anymore."

"That's right," Dana said. "Daddy can't move his arms."

"And Daddy can't run around anymore," Will continued.

"That's right; he can't."

Then he paused, screwed up his face in concentration and burst out happily, "But he can still smile."

On June 5 I had my operation. It was a success. My doctor predicted that with time I ought to be able to get off the respirator and breathe on my own.

Three weeks later I moved to the Kessler Institute for Rehabilitation in West Orange, New Jersey. The worst days there were when Bill Carroll, the respiratory therapist, would test my vital capacity, a measure of how much air I could move on my own. I was failing miserably. To even consider weaning yourself off the ventilator, you need a vital capacity of about 750 c.c.'s, but I could hardly move the needle above zero.

At about this time I had to decide if I would attend the annual fund-raising dinner of the Creative Coalition, an organization of people in the arts. The dinner was scheduled for October 16 at the Pierre Hotel in New York City. I felt obligated to go, especially because Robin Williams was to be honored for his charitable work.

Still, I worried about making the trip into Manhattan. It would be the first time I would be in public since my accident in May. Would my muscles go into a spasm as they often did? Would I have a pop-off?

Dana and I talked it over and decided that the psychological advantages of going outweighed the physical risks. We dusted off my tuxedo, and on the afternoon of the 16th, I braced myself for the unknown.

For nearly five months I'd been cruising in a wheelchair at three miles an hour. Now I was strapped in the back of a van driving into the city at 55 miles an hour. As we hit bumps and potholes, my neck froze with tension, and my body was racked with spasms.

Once at the hotel, I was quickly transferred to a suite with a hospital bed to rest. The whole experience was more intense than I had anticipated.

At last it was time for me to present Robin with his award. For a split second I wished a genie could make me disappear. As I was pushed onto the stage, though, I looked out to see 700 people on their feet, cheering. The ovation went on for more than five minutes.

From that moment on, the evening was transformed into a celebration of friendship. Later, as we bounced through the Lincoln Tunnel back to New Jersey, I was so excited I hardly noticed the rough ride. Back at Kessler, Dana produced a bottle of chardonnay, and we toasted a milestone in my new life. I'd made it!

I MADE up my mind—I wanted to breathe on my own again.

On November 2 Bill Carroll, two doctors and a physical therapist brought in the breathing equipment, took me off the ventilator and asked me to take ten breaths.

Lying on my back, I was gasping, my eyes rolling up in my head. With each attempt I was only able to draw in an average of 50 c.c.'s. But at least I had moved the dial.

The next day I told myself over and over that I was going home soon, and imagined my chest as a huge bellows that I could open and close at will. I took the ten breaths, and my average was 450 c.c.'s. *Now we're getting somewhere,* I thought.

The following day my average was 560 c.c.'s. A cheer broke out. "I've never seen progress like that," Carroll said. "You're going to get off this thing."

After that I practiced every day. I went from seven minutes off the ventilator to 12 minutes to 15. Just before I left Kessler, I gave it everything I had and breathed for 30 minutes on my own.

I'M HAPPY that I decided to keep living, and so are those who are close to me. On Thanksgiving, 1995, I went home to spend the day with my family for the first time since the accident. When I saw our home again, I wept as Dana held me. At the dinner table each of us spoke a few words about what we were thankful for.

Will said simply, "Dad." 🕊

Life in These United States

WHEN OUR last child moved out, my wife encouraged me to join Big Brothers. I was matched with a 13-year-old named Alex. Our first outing was to the library, where we ran into his friend.

"Who's he?" the friend asked Alex, pointing to me.

"My Big Brother, Randall."

The boy looked at me, then back at Alex. "Dude, how old is your mother?"   *Randall Martin*

His Gift of the Future

BY MARC LERNER

June 1995

THE ENVELOPE bore the return address of a social-welfare center in Seoul. Inside was a thick autobiography written by a Korean War refugee named Yang-chin Chi. He wondered if his story might interest my editors.

I had my doubts, but as I began scanning the pages, I found myself intrigued. Then I came to the lines that hooked me: "I felt incredible frustration, and my determination seemed to fade. It was at this desperate time in my life that I met Dr. Roy L. Thomas." What followed was a description of an extraordinary friendship that blossomed between a black U.S. Army surgeon and a destitute Korean boy.

I wanted to know more, and that is how I found myself, on a breezy afternoon last summer, sitting with Yang-chin Chi on the patio outside his home in Seoul. "It goes back a long time," the lanky 57-year-old professor told me, "and some of it is very sad. . . ."

FOR 13 generations, the Chi family had tilled the hillsides of Gwi-nae, a tiny village on Korea's Yellow Sea coast. It was there, on October 13, 1936, that Yang-chin Chi was born. As a child, Chi sat spellbound while his grandfather, a teacher, entertained him with tales of Asian history.

Chi longed to pursue formal schooling himself. But disease and war conspired against his dream. Chi's father died of tuberculosis in 1945, and by then all the family savings had been used up in his treatment.

Realizing Chi's passion for learning, his mother let him board with another family and attend the nearest school, 20 miles away. But on weekends he trekked home to hitch a yoke to the family cow and help his two brothers and two sisters cultivate the rice paddies.

On one of these trips home, Chi's life fell out from under him. A few hours after midnight on June 25, 1950, Communist North Korean troops swarmed across the border 20 miles away. A full-scale attack on U.S.-backed South Korea was under way.

THE CHI family fled to desolate Soonwee Island, 2½ miles off the coast. They cut a cave into a hillside and scavenged for food and firewood.

By January 1952, North Korean troops had begun forays near Soonwee, and the time had come to flee again. The Chi family joined a throng on the beach and tried to find room aboard one of the boats escaping south.

One afternoon Chi and his older brother, Moon-ok, managed to wedge themselves aboard a packed 20-foot boat, but they couldn't squeeze any more room. Moon-ok stuffed a tiny wad of Korean money into his brother's pocket. "You must go," he shouted above crashing breakers. "If you survive, at least one member of the family can carry on." Then he jumped off.

The ramshackle vessel pulled away. Chi could only look back on the beach and wail in sorrow. It was the last glimpse he ever had of his family.

A U.S. NAVY ship took the boat refugees to Korea's southwestern coast. Chi hitched a ride to the city of Pusan, where he found work feeding wounded soldiers. He also took English and math classes at the YMCA.

Alone and afraid, Chi calmed his mind by focusing on his dream. *I have to get a better education,* he told himself. *That will be my goal.*

Chi found further solace in assuring himself that he would one day see his family again. But when the war ended with an uneasy truce on July 27, 1953, the new demarcation line between North and South Korea placed Chi's native village squarely in Communist territory. A journey home was now impossible.

Chi moved to Seoul, where he hoped for more opportunities. He earned his high-school diploma and resolved to somehow get a university degree. *I have nothing left except what I can build with my mind,* he thought. But having little money, he harbored a smothering fear that fate had snatched away his dream.

Chi found work as a houseboy at a U.S.-Korean military base in Il-dong, north of Seoul. There, in April 1955, he watched as a stocky black man with a thin mustache stepped from a jeep and dusted off his captain's uniform. Chi scooped up the officer's duffel bags.

"I'm Dr. Roy Thomas," the man said in a quiet, soothing voice.

Along the way to the VIP quarters, Dr. Thomas chatted with Chi, asking him about his duties. *I am just a lowly houseboy, and yet he wants to know about me,* Chi thought.

As chief medical officer at Il-dong, the 33-year-old surgeon was burdened with work, yet he always spared time for Chi. When the young man struggled to express himself in English, the doctor encouraged him to write down the words.

Eventually Dr. Thomas became Chi's language coach. He listened while Chi recited English aphorisms: "Poverty saves one thousand times more men than it ruins," "Every cloud has a silver lining," "Time and tide wait for no man." Dr. Thomas used these simple sayings to reinforce the idea that nothing was impossible if Chi worked hard enough.

During lesson breaks, Dr. Thomas asked Chi about his life and was clearly moved. In turn, Chi learned about the doctor's past.

Roy Thomas was born in Youngstown, Ohio, to a struggling family that had migrated from Greenwood, Mississippi. His parents had had little schooling and placed the highest premium on education. Young Roy followed their counsel, completing medical school on the Army's tab. When called to Korea, Thomas left behind a wife and two children—an eight-year-old boy and a six-year-old girl.

A few months after they met, Chi sought out his new friend. "Captain Thomas, I'll never make it to university if I continue to live in this remote area," he said. "I must find work in Seoul."

The doctor agreed, putting a hand on the young man's shoulder. "If you work hard, Mr. Chi, I'm sure all will turn out well." He made Chi promise to send his address in Seoul.

Back in the capital, Chi worked as a waiter in an Army officers club. But the pay was poor, and he soon found his spirits slumping. *How can I ever save up enough to enter college?* he wondered.

One October morning Chi was stunned to see Dr. Thomas striding into the club. The surgeon went over to Chi's supervisor to get permission for the young man to take the rest of the day off.

"Are you still serious about attending university?" Dr. Thomas asked. Chi nodded. "Come with me, then," the doctor said. "There's a place we should visit."

They hopped into a jeep and drove to the rolling campus of Seoul National University. "You belong at a school like this, Mr. Chi," Dr. Thomas said.

As they walked around the grounds, Dr. Thomas told Chi more about his own education. "After high school I wanted to work in the steel mills." But a family friend who had graduated from Morehouse College in Atlanta convinced Thomas of the value of a degree from the renowned black college. In September 1940 he entered Morehouse and was soon in its premed program.

Becoming a doctor was no easy thing for a young black man in the 1940s, Thomas added. Few hospitals in the country were open to black interns and residents. But he wouldn't let prejudice defeat him and earned his degree from Meharry Medical College, a black school in Nashville.

His challenges as a black man gave him empathy for Chi and his struggles. "Believe in yourself," he told

Chi. "And don't give up until you've achieved your goals."

When Dr. Thomas dropped him off that night, Chi learned that his friend's tour in Korea would soon be up. The two would likely never meet again. "Good luck to you, Mr. Chi," the doctor said quietly. Overcome, the young Korean clasped his friend's hand. Long after Dr. Thomas had driven off, Chi stood at his doorway, staring into the darkness.

LETTERS SOON started arriving from America, all carefully printed in large block letters for Chi to easily decipher, and all filled with the gentle prodding one might expect from a loving parent. Chi read and reread them until they were nearly worn through.

"Remember," Dr. Thomas wrote in one note, "the hardships of your youth will turn out to be a valuable experience. The iron tempered in a forge is stronger than one that never faced the forge."

Each letter ended with the same sentence, underlined in bold red ink: "Do you still plan to attend university next spring?"

Only at a friend's insistence, however, did Chi take the admission test for Seoul's Chung-Ang University. *It's a vain exercise,* he told himself. The tuition deadline was in eight weeks and, with his meager earnings, he had no chance of coming up with the $85 he needed.

His frustration soared when he learned that he'd passed with high grades. His university admission was guaranteed—if only he had the funds. Chi decided to let the doctor know of his admission to Chung-Ang and mentioned the difficulty of the high tuition costs.

Six weeks later, a letter arrived from the United States. Chi was flabbergasted to find four twenty-dollar bills and one five-dollar bill inside. The money was, Dr. Thomas wrote, "a congratulatory gift." In April 1956 Yang-chin Chi, now 19, entered college.

FOR A time, Chi kept his American friend apprised of his academic progress. But as their lives grew hectic, the correspondence began to trail off.

Chi earned his undergraduate degree in English language and literature, then went into social work, becoming an orphanage director.

In the late 1960s Chi won a Fulbright scholarship in America, receiving a master's degree in social work from the University of Wisconsin in Milwaukee. He had one short phone conversation with Dr. Thomas, but the surgeon moved soon thereafter and the two men lost touch. Eventually, Chi returned to his alma mater, Chung-Ang University, as a professor.

In November 1975 Chi founded South Korea's first private social-welfare center for the poor. And thanks to Chi's work, the Chung-Ang University Social Welfare Center has become a model for several other centers across Korea. Then he began working with the United Nations agency UNICEF in Korea and other countries. Within a few more years, he obtained a Ph.D. in social work from the University of Sussex in Brighton, England. The boy who had almost given up on his education had become a renowned scholar.

As the years passed and his professional successes mounted, Chi found himself thinking often of Dr. Thomas. In April 1992, when he and his wife and three children watched horrifying television coverage of the Los Angeles race riots, he felt an overwhelming sadness, hearing of the tensions between American blacks and Koreans. *How can this be when Dr. Thomas and I could so easily reach across the boundaries of race and culture?*

"I HOPE I can meet him again someday," Chi told me when we met in Seoul. "Dr. Thomas brought me through a time in my life when all I had was his helping hand."

I left Chi determined to assist him in his search for his old friend. I contacted the Ohio State Medical Association—no listing. There was nothing in the databanks of black-physician organizations. As a passing thought, I asked the American Medical Association if it kept separate data on retired doctors. It did. Before long, a St. Louis address turned up for a retired physician by that name. I telephoned.

A soft, hesitant voice answered: "Yes, I am Dr. Roy Thomas. Who's calling?" I explained.

"I remember Mr. Chi," Dr. Thomas said. "But I did so little for him, and it was so many years ago. I'm surprised he even remembers me."

A few weeks later, sitting with Dr. Thomas and his wife in their St. Louis apartment, I told him how his simple acts of kindness had opened up Chi's life and how he was now a leading voice on social welfare in his country. "He credits you for all of this," I noted.

"I don't understand," Dr. Thomas said. "I'm glad to know my assistance helped, but he succeeded because of who he was—not because of me."

I knew Dr. Thomas was wrong. What had seemed like insignificant gestures to him had proved to be something quite different to a poor Korean boy alone in the world. They were the gift that gave Yang-chin Chi a future.

ON AN evening last July Chi excitedly dialed the phone number I had passed along to him. In seconds, he was talking to Dr. Thomas, across nearly 7,000 miles, nine time zones and so many years.

"It is a miracle I have found you after such a long time," Chi said, laughing. "I had almost given up."

The two discussed the many turns their lives had taken since their time in Korea. Chi recounted his accomplishments for his old mentor.

"My friend," Dr. Thomas said, "I'm so proud to see what you've made of yourself. I always knew it was there inside of you."

Chi paused as he searched for just the right words.

"I want you to know something," the Korean said in a voice that shook with emotion. "Meeting you was one of the most significant moments in my life. Our friendship was a turning point for me."

Then, after waiting so many years for his chance, Chi finally spoke the words he had long held in his heart.

"Dr. Thomas—thank you."

Money Talk

MONEY IS a singular thing. It ranks with love as man's greatest source of joy. And with death as his greatest source of anxiety. *John Kenneth Galbraith*

• • •

IT IS said that for money you can have everything, but you cannot. You can buy food, but not appetite; medicine, but not health; knowledge, but not wisdom; glitter, but not beauty; fun, but not joy; acquaintances, but not friends; servants, but not faithfulness; leisure, but not peace. You can have the husk of everything for money, but not the kernel. *Arne Garborg*

A Heart for the Run

GARY PAULSEN

April 1997

FROM *Puppies, Dogs, and Blue Northers*

COOKIE HAD been my lead sled dog for close to 14,000 miles, including an Iditarod, the nearly 1,200-mile race from Anchorage to Nome, Alaska. Several times she saved my life. Somewhere along the way she became more than a dog, more than a friend—almost my alter ego.

Now she was due to give birth in a wild winter storm, and my anxiety was acute. I thought of bringing her from the kennel into our small log house in northern Minnesota, but it would be too warm. Her coat was in full prime—she was at least a third wolf with gray wolf markings—and the heat would be murderous.

I decided to construct an igloolike hut from bales of straw I kept near the kennel. It was just big enough for Cookie—and me, since the only way I could get any relief from my worry was to stay with her. Once inside, I crawled into my sleeping bag and said to Cookie, "Nice. Way better than we're used to."

She was busy licking herself and didn't respond, although she usually did. We talked often. I frequently explained parts of my life to her, which sometimes helped me better understand myself.

I fell asleep and awakened four hours later to find Cookie giving birth. Four gray pups making small whine-grunt sounds were out and cleaned.

Everything went fine until the eighth and last pup. It was stillborn. Cookie worked at it, licking harder and harder, trying to get it to breathe, her actions becoming frantic.

She growled concern, and it turned to a whine. I reached one hand to cover her eyes, and with the other took the pup and buried it under some straw near the door opening. With other females I had hidden the dead pup to take away later, and it had worked. The mother focused on the live pups and forgot the dead one.

But I should have known better. This was Cookie—stubborn, immensely strong-willed and powerful, completely dedicated to those she loved.

She looked for the pup, and when she couldn't find it, she looked me in the eye. *Where is it?*

I reached under the straw, and she took it gently in her mouth, set it down and began working on it again. When she could not get it to respond, she put it with the other nursing pups.

The movement of the pups caused the body of the dead one to move. She must have thought it alive, because she lay back exhausted from the birthing, closed her eyes and went to sleep. I waited a full minute, then carefully removed the dead pup and took it outside to a snowbank 20 yards away. Pushing it into the snow, I covered it, then stole back to our shelter, got into my sleeping bag and slept.

When I awakened, Cookie was still asleep. I was getting ready to leave when something stopped me.

There in the middle of the puppies lay the dead pup, stuck into a nursing position. Without awakening me, Cookie had gotten up and found it.

I was caught between heartbreak and admiration. Again I thought I would take the pup while Cookie slept. But when I reached across to get it, her eyes opened and her lips curled. Again she looked into my eyes.

Almost four days passed before she finally let me take her dead puppy. But even then she growled, not at me, but at the fates that would have her lose a young one.

I HAD another demonstration of Cookie's devotion on a nighttime winter run. It was clear, 15 or 20 degrees below zero, with a full moon. I put her at the front of the team with three of the seasoned dogs and six of her now nearly grown pups behind, a total of ten dogs.

I planned to run 100 miles along abandoned railroad tracks that had been converted to a wilderness trail. The tracks and ties had been removed, and the old trestle bridges had been resurfaced with thick plywood.

Twenty-five miles into the run we started across a trestle over a river. In the middle of the trestle, 20 feet above the river, the dogs suddenly stopped. Some maniac had stolen the plywood that provided a base for the snow on the trestle.

I jammed the two steel teeth of my snow brake. But instead of sliding on the plywood to a gradual stop, the teeth caught on an open crosstie and stopped the sled with a jolt.

I slammed into the handlebar with my stomach, flew over the sled and dropped headfirst into a snowbank next to the river. I hit perfectly. If I had landed in the river, I would have drowned or frozen. If I had struck ice, I would have broken my neck.

As I struggled to my feet, I saw Cookie waiting on the trestle above, the team lined behind her, each dog on a tie with open space between them. I couldn't turn them around without getting them tangled. Nor could I drive them over the trestle in the harness; the younger ones could fall between the ties.

"I can't do anything," I said to Cookie.

She stared back at me. *You got us into this,* her eyes said, *and you'd better get us out.*

I climbed up the bank to the trestle and began to release the dogs one at a time. Each crossed the trestle, moving carefully from tie to tie. On the other side they didn't stop. The older dogs had been here before and knew the way home. The pups followed. Soon they vanished in the night.

"Well," I said to Cookie, "it's you and me."

I let her loose and in disbelief watched her take off after the team. "Traitor," I said with great feeling.

I managed to drag the sled off the trestle. Once on solid ground, I trudged along with the sled behind me, feeling as if I were on a treadmill. With some 30 miles to go, it would take three days to get home.

After about 40 minutes I heard a sound. Minto, a large, red dog, came up and sat down facing me.

"Hello," I said. "Get lonely?" As I was rubbing his ears, another dog, Winston, trotted up.

"What is this?" I said. "Loyalty?"

The truth was, they shouldn't have been there. Race teams are trained for only one thing: to go and never stop. They do not come back. But four more did, then one more, then the last two pups and, finally, Cookie.

I hooked them up and managed to get a "thank

you" past the lump in my throat. As I drove them forward, I noticed that some of the dogs had slight bite wounds on the ends of their ears.

Sitting in the kitchen later, I said to my wife, Ruth, "It sounds insane, but it looked like Cookie went after them and sent them back. I've never heard anything like it."

"I know one thing," Ruth replied. "You aren't paying her nearly enough."

COOKIE AND I had to retire from racing at around the same time. Arthritis in her ankles sidelined her. Then one day, breaking up a dogfight, I felt a sudden pain in my chest. The doctor said I had heart disease.

I found someone to take the other dogs and moved Cookie into the house. She stayed with me constantly, sitting next to me on the couch to watch TV and growling whenever a cat or dog came on.

Diet, medication and exercise helped me, and I became more active. On the first hard fall morning I went out to the woodpile to split kindling, Cookie by my side. At the pile I stopped, but she kept going.

I knew what she was thinking. Long runs, towing a wheeled sled, had always come with first cold. Cookie had loved them.

I found her at the precise spot in the kennel where she'd stood hundreds of times, waiting for the team to be hooked up.

"No," I said, coming up next to her. "We don't do that now."

She whined softly.

I walked toward the woodpile. I did not dare look back, or I would have lost it. As always, her determination to be with me won out even over the call of the trail. When she caught up to me, I reached down to pet her. She leaned against my leg.

TWO MORE summers and one more winter came and went. Cookie stayed by my side.

Then one morning in late summer I let her out, and she did not come back for breakfast. I found her under a spruce tree, dead, her face to the east, her eyes half-open.

I sat next to her crying. Then I took her back to the place in the kennel where she loved to stand, the place where we harnessed. I buried her there with her collar still on, bearing the little metal tag with the number 32—her number, and mine, in the Iditarod.

I thought of when she was young and there was nothing in front of us but the iceblink on the horizon. I hoped that wherever dogs go, she would find, now and then, a good run. 🦢

The Gratitude Club

BY STEVE HARTMAN

July/August 2012

FROM THE CBS News Archives

I've been reporting on extraordinary people for 25 years as a television journalist, but this small Oregon town and the man at its center, Woody Davis, stand alone in my memory.

When I read a newspaper clip about the community's reaction to Woody's declining health, I knew that this would be a special story for my CBS Evening News series, On the Road *(the transcript of which is below). But nothing prepared me for what happened when I traveled to Oregon last December and began knocking on doors. Every single person knew Woody and had count-*

less stories to tell about his selflessness and generosity.

For five decades, he had helped plow cars out of snow, chopped wood, repaired farm equipment and more. He was the consummate good neighbor, and in his time of need, the community was rallying around him. I'd never seen anything like it.

Corbett, Oregon, December 2011—On a high ridge above the Columbia River, just down from heaven, you'll find an angel on a front-end loader.

Woody Davis, 69, is kind of a jack-of-all-trades. And although he's never made much money at it, by all accounts, he has earned his wings.

Here is some of what people in town have said of him:

"He's the epitome of something dear."

"You have to chase him down to pay him sometimes."

"He's uncommon, he's special, he's a gift that this community has had all these years."

Which is why folks in this small town east of Portland are now going out of their way to thank Woody for the thousands of good deeds he's done for them over the past 50 years.

Recently, they all got together to cut and stack his firewood for winter. A couple of guys fixed up his old pickup. Someone even built him a beautiful wooden box and invited the whole town to sign it.

"Did you know how much the community cared for him?" I asked Woody's son, Clint.

"Not to the degree I do now," he said.

Clint said all the work his dad did for people has been repaid tenfold. "Bill Gates could not come to Corbett and buy this. You can't buy the love that people have poured out for Dad."

Their words and deeds are sincere and lasting. Unfortunately, the box is pine—and the outlook isn't good.

A few months ago, Woody was diagnosed with ALS—Lou Gehrig's disease. Doctors tell him he has about six months. The disease, which attacks the nervous system, is already making it hard for him to lift much of anything or even talk. But his attitude remains unaffected.

"What do you think of what everybody's been doing for you?" I asked.

"I feel blessed that I'm dying slowly."

I really didn't think I'd heard him right. "Wait, did you just say you feel blessed that you're dying slowly?"

"Because people have a chance to express to me how they feel," he said.

In most communities, death is whispered, and praise is saved for the eulogy. But Woody Davis and the people of Corbett, Oregon, show us why that may be too late. Turns out even angels like to know they've made a difference. 🕊

Giving
Giving
Giving
Giving

The Christmas Present

BY JAMES A. MICHENER

December 1967

WHEN I was a boy of nine in the little town of Doylestown, Pennsylvania, I used to mow the lawn of Mrs. Long, an elderly lady who lived across from the Presbyterian Church. She paid me very little for the chore, which was not surprising for she had not much money. But she did promise me, "When Christmas comes I shall have a present for you." And she said this with such enthusiasm that I felt assured the present would be magnificent.

I spent much time wondering what it would be.

The boys I played with had baseball gloves and bicycles and ice skates, and I was so eager to acquire any one of these things that I convinced myself that my benefactor intended choosing from among them.

"It would hardly be a baseball glove," I reasoned with myself. "A woman like Mrs. Long wouldn't know much about baseball." Since she was a frail little person I also ruled out the bicycle, for how could she handle such a contraption?

On my last Saturday at work Mrs. Long said, "Now remember, because you've been a good boy all summer, at Christmas I'll have a present waiting. You come to the door and collect it." These words clinched it. Since she was going to have the present in her house, and since she herself would be handling it, unquestionably she was giving me a pair of ice skates.

So convinced of this I became that I could see the skates and imagine myself upon them. As the cold days of November arrived and ice began to form on the ponds which were then a feature of rural Doylestown, I began to try my luck on the ice that would be sustaining me and my skates through the winter.

"Get away from the ice!" a man shouted. "It's not strong enough yet." But soon it would be.

AS CHRISTMAS approached, it was with difficulty that I restrained myself from reporting to Mrs. Long and demanding my present. Our family agreed that the first of December was too early for me to do this. "She may not have it wrapped yet," someone argued, and this made sense. But the 15th was also too early, and the 20th, too. I argued back on the 20th, reasoning that if I was going to get a present I might as well get it now, but my mother pointed out that in our family we never opened our presents until Christmas morning.

On the 21st of December, a serious cold snap froze all the ponds so the boys who already had ice skates were able to use them, and my longing to possess mine, even though I could not open the package for a few days, became overpowering. On December 22nd I could restrain myself no longer. I marched down the street, presented myself at the door of the house whose lawn I had tended all summer and said, "I've come for my present, Mrs. Long."

"I've been waiting for you," she said, leading me into her parlor, its windows heavy with purple velvet. She sat me in a chair, disappeared to another room, and in a moment stood before me holding a package which under no conceivable circumstances could hold a baseball glove or a bicycle or even a pair of skates. I was painfully disappointed but so far as I can recall did not show it, because during the week my advisers at home had warned repeatedly, "Whatever she has for you, take it graciously and say thank you."

What she had was an ordinary parcel about 22

centimeters wide, 30 centimeters long and no more than 8 millimeters thick. As Mrs. Long held it in her frail hands, curiosity replaced my initial disappointment, and when I lifted it from her the extreme lightness of the gift quite captivated me. It weighed almost nothing.

"What is it?" I asked.

"You'll see on Christmas Day."

I shook it. Nothing rattled, but I thought I did catch a sound of some sort—a quiet, muffled sound that was somehow familiar but unidentifiable. "What is it?" I asked again.

"A kind of magic," Mrs. Long said, and that was all.

Her words were enough to set my mind dancing with new possibilities, so that by the time I reached home I had convinced myself that I held some great wonder. "She gave me a magician's set. I'll turn pitchers of milk into rabbits."

How long the passage to Christmas was! There were other presents of normal dimension and weight. But Mrs. Long's box dominated all, for it had to do with magic.

ON CHRISTMAS morning, before the sun was up. I had this box on my knees, tearing at the reused colored string which bound it. Soon the wrapping paper was off and in my lap lay a flat box with its top hinged about halfway down.

With great excitement I opened the hinged lid to find inside a shimmering pile of ten flimsy sheets of black paper, each labeled in iridescent letters, Carbon Paper Regal Premium. Of the four words I knew only the second, and what it signified in this context I could not guess. Vaguely I remembered that the present had something to do with magic, and with this word on my lips I turned to the elders who had watched me unwrapping my gift.

"Is it magic?" I asked.

Aunt Laura, who taught school, had the presence of mind to say, "It really is!" And she took two pieces of white paper, placed between them one of the black sheets from the box and, with a hard pencil, wrote my name on the upper sheet. Then, removing it and the Carbon Paper Regal Premium, she handed me the second sheet, which her pencil had in no way touched.

There was my name! It was clean, and very dark, and well formed and as beautiful as Christmas Day itself.

I was enthralled! This was indeed magic ... of the greatest dimension. That a pencil could write on one piece of paper and mysteriously record on another was a miracle which was so gratifying to my childish mind that I can honestly say that in that one moment, in the dark of Christmas morning, I understood as much about printing, and the duplication of words, and the fundamental mystery of disseminating ideas as I have learned in the remaining half-century of my life.

I WROTE and wrote, using up whole tablets until I had ground off the last shred of blackness from the ten sheets of carbon paper. It was the most enchanting Christmas present a boy like me could have had, infinitely more significant than a baseball glove or a pair of skates. It was exactly the present I needed and it reached me at precisely that Christmas when I was best able to comprehend it. Because it enabled me to learn something about the reproduction of words, it opened vast portals of imagination.

I have received some pretty thundering Christmas presents since then, but none ever came close to the magnificence of this one. The average present merely gratifies a temporary yearning, as the ice skates would have done; the great present illuminates all the years of life that remain.

It was not until some years later that I realized that the ten sheets of Carbon Paper Regal Premium which Mrs. Long gave me had cost her nothing. She had used them for her purposes and would normally have thrown them away, except that she had the ingenuity to guess that a boy might profit from a present totally outside the realm of his ordinary experience. Although she had spent no money on me, she had spent something infinitely more valuable: imagination.

I hope that each year some boys and girls, will receive, from thoughtful adults who really love them, gifts which will jolt them out of all they have known up to now. It is such gifts and such experiences—usually costing little or nothing—that transform a life and lend it an impetus that may continue for decades. 🕊

Laughter, the Best Medicine

THE DEVOUT cowboy lost his favorite Bible while he was mending fences out on the range.

Three weeks later a cow walked up to him carrying the Bible in its mouth. The cowboy couldn't believe his eyes. He took the book out of the cow's mouth, raised his eyes heavenward and exclaimed, "It's a miracle!"

"Not really," said the cow. "Your name is written inside the cover."   *Roman Wilbert*

• • •

A FARMER pulls a prank on Easter Sunday. After the egg hunt, he sneaks into the chicken coop and replaces every white egg with a brightly colored one. Minutes later, the rooster walks in. He spots the colored eggs, then storms out and beats up the peacock.   *Adam Joshua Smargon*

The Man on the Train

BY ALEX HALEY

February 1991

WHENEVER MY brothers, sister and I get together we inevitably talk about Dad. We all owe our success in life to him—and to a mysterious man he met one night on a train.

Our father, Simon Alexander Haley, was born in 1892 and reared in the small farming town of Savannah, Tennessee. He was the eighth child of Alec Haley—a tough-willed former slave and part-time sharecropper—and of a woman named Queen.

Although sensitive and emotional, my grandmother could be tough-willed herself, especially when it came to her children. One of her ambitions was that my father be educated.

Back then in Savannah a boy was considered "wasted" if he remained in school after he was big enough to do farm work. So when my father reached the sixth grade, Queen began massaging grandfather's ego.

"Since we have eight children," she would argue, "wouldn't it be prestigious if we deliberately *wasted* one and got him educated?" After many arguments, Grandfather let Dad finish the eighth grade. Still, he had to work in the fields after school.

But Queen was not satisfied. As eighth grade ended, she began planting seeds, saying Grandfather's image would reach new heights if their son went to high school.

Her barrage worked. Stern old Alec Haley handed my father five hard-earned ten-dollar bills, told him never to ask for more and sent him off to high school. Traveling first by mule cart and then by train—the first train he had ever seen—Dad finally alighted in Jackson, Tennessee, where he enrolled in the preparatory department of Lane College. The black Methodist school offered courses up through junior college.

Dad's $50 was soon used up, and to continue in school, he worked as a waiter, a handyman and a helper at a school for wayward boys. And when winter came, he'd arise at 4 a.m., go into prosperous white families' homes and make fires so the residents would awaken in comfort.

Poor Simon became something of a campus joke with his one pair of pants and shoes, and his droopy eyes. Often he was found asleep with a textbook fallen into his lap.

The constant struggle to earn money took its toll. Dad's grades began to flounder. But he pushed onward and completed senior high. Next he enrolled in A & T College in Greensboro, North Carolina, a land-grant school where he struggled through freshman and sophomore years.

One bleak afternoon at the close of his second year, Dad was called into a teacher's office and told that he'd failed a course—one that required a textbook he'd been too poor to buy.

A ponderous sense of defeat descended upon him. For years he'd given his utmost, and now he felt he had accomplished nothing. Maybe he should return home to his original destiny of sharecropping.

But days later, a letter came from the Pullman Company saying he was one of 24 black college men selected from hundreds of applicants to be summer-time sleeping-car porters. Dad was ecstatic. Here was a chance! He eagerly reported for duty and was assigned a Buffalo-to-Pittsburgh train.

The train was racketing along one morning about 2 a.m. when the porter's buzz sounded. Dad sprang up, jerked on his white jacket and made his way to the passenger berths. There a distinguished-looking man said he and his wife were having trouble sleeping and they both wanted glasses of warm milk. Dad brought milk and napkins on a silver tray. The man handed one glass through the lower-berth curtains to his wife and, sipping from his own glass, began to engage Dad in conversation.

Pullman Company rules strictly prohibited any conversation beyond "Yes, sir" or "No, ma'am," but this passenger kept asking questions. He even followed Dad back into the porter's cubicle.

"Where are you from?"

"Savannah, Tennessee, sir."

"You speak quite well."

"Thank you, sir."

"What work did you do before this?"

"I'm a student at A & T College in Greensboro, sir." Dad felt no need to add that he was considering returning home to sharecrop.

The man looked at him keenly, finally wished him well and returned to his bunk.

The next morning, the train reached Pittsburgh. At a time when 50 cents was a good tip, the man gave five dollars to Simon Haley, who was profusely grateful. All summer, he had been saving every tip he received, and when the job finally ended, he had accumulated enough to buy his own mule and plow. But he realized his savings could also pay for one full semester at A & T without his having to work a single odd job.

Dad decided he deserved at least one semester free of outside work. Only that way would he know what grades he could truly achieve.

He returned to Greensboro. But no sooner did he arrive on campus than he was summoned by the college president. Dad was full of apprehension as he seated himself before the great man.

"I have a letter here, Simon," the president said.

"Yes, sir."

"You were a porter for Pullman this summer?"

"Yes, sir."

"Did you meet a certain man one night and bring him warm milk?"

"Yes, sir."

"Well, his name is Mr. R. S. M. Boyce, and he's a retired executive of the Curtis Publishing Company, which publishes *The Saturday Evening Post*. He has donated $500 for your board, tuition and books for the entire school year."

My father was astonished.

The surprise grant not only enabled Dad to finish A & T, but to graduate first in his class. And that achievement earned him a full scholarship to Cornell University in Ithaca, New York.

In 1920, Dad, then a newlywed, moved to Ithaca with his bride, Bertha. He entered Cornell to pursue his Master's degree, and my mother enrolled at the Ithaca Conservatory of Music to study piano. I was born the following year.

One day decades later, editors of *The Saturday Evening Post* invited me to their editorial offices in New York to discuss the condensation of my first book, *The Autobiography of Malcolm X.* I was so proud, so happy, to be sitting in those wood-paneled offices on Lexington Avenue. Suddenly I remembered Mr. Boyce, and how it was his generosity that enabled me to be there amid those editors, as a writer. And then I began to cry. I just couldn't help it.

We children of Simon Haley often reflect on Mr. Boyce and his investment in a less fortunate human being. By the ripple effect of his generosity, we also benefited. Instead of being raised on a sharecrop farm, we grew up in a home with educated parents, shelves full of books, and with pride in ourselves. My brother George is chairman of the U.S. Postal Rate Commission, Julius is an architect, Lois a music teacher and I'm a writer.

Mr. R.S.M. Boyce dropped like a blessing into my father's life. What some may see as a chance encounter, I see as the working of a mysterious power for good.

And I believe that each person blessed with success has an obligation to return part of that blessing. We must all live and act like the man on the train. 🕊

Ferragamo's Gift

BY SUSAN SHREVE

August 2003

FROM *More*

WANDERING ALONG the streets of New York City, my daughters and I stop at shoe stores from the Village to the Upper West Side—wherever we happen to be. This is their choice, these women who as little girls teetered around the house balancing like cranes in my mother's high heels. I sit on a bench and wait while they try on shoe after shoe, readjusting their positions in the mirror, eyes downcast, considering their feet.

"So?" one of them will ask me. "What do you think of these?"

"I love them." I say this about every pair, of course. Which isn't true. I have a complicated relationship with shoes. Given a choice—which a mother of two daughters on a shopping spree doesn't necessarily have—I'd never go into a shoe store at all.

But my mother would be ecstatic. In the romance of shoes, they are my mother's daughters.

I am her true daughter—and growing up I was her full-time job, one she took on with grace. I'd had polio as a baby, and learned to walk in braces wearing heavy, brown orthopedic oxfords. The fact that they were not the black patent Mary Janes the other little girls were wearing concerned me less than it did my mother, who was in love with shoes.

There was an element of boot camp to my early childhood: posture exercises, ballet school run by a French dancer who wasn't enthusiastic at the arrival of a hopeful ballerina wearing oxfords and a metal brace. My mother bought me ballet slippers. I couldn't walk in them. But I held tight to the barre, pretending I could leap, my legs in perfect half-moons, my pink slippers pointed.

By the time I was seven, my mother had moved on to tennis, which she decided I could play while wearing black rain rubbers over my oxfords. And long before anyone in my class had heard of ballroom dancing, my mother played swing music on the phonograph in the living room, took me in her arms and taught me how.

By age 12, after a series of operations, I could walk unaided. When I turned 15, she signed me up for dancing school with boys. She took me shopping at the Washington's Birthday sales, buying me a sliplike dress with a deep V and a strapless satiny thing. But shoes were a dilemma: I wore two sizes, one 5½, the other 3.

"I can't wear these to dancing school," I said of my orthopedics.

"Of course not," my mother agreed. "We'll buy you heels."

So we went to G.C. Murphy's Five and Ten and bought a pair of size 5½, stuffing one shoe with toilet paper so it would fit my smaller foot.

I wore the satiny formal to the first dance. I managed to take a turn with a boy so tall I couldn't see his face—which was just as well, since the toilet paper began to trail in a long ribbon across the dance floor. I fled the studio and hid in the ladies' room—my feet up on the toilet seat so no one could see I was there—until dancing school was over. I never went back.

"We'll find you shoes," my mother promised me that night.

"I don't need to go to dances," I said.

"Maybe not," she answered. "But you need to have the shoes, in case you change your mind."

Someplace in my mother's fashion-magazine reading, she recalled that Salvatore Ferragamo had a child with polio. She wrote to him, saying that she, too, had such a child, telling him the story of the dance. Would he consider making my shoes?

By this time, Ferragamo was well known as a shoemaker, with rich clients all over the world. But my mother was certain he would write back. And he did, inviting us to Florence, offering to make a "last"— a model of my foot—at no cost.

Ferragamo died before we could get to Florence. As it turned out, he did not have a child with polio. But he was a sympathetic man, and his wife and daughters honored his letter.

And so it was that as an awkward, self-conscious teenager, I sat at the Palazzo Spini Feroni headquarters next to my lovely mother and was measured. What I remember about that afternoon—besides the slender models walking the marble floors and the elegant women sampling the wares—is the sense I had of my mother. She commanded the room in her quiet way, as if she had brought to Florence a precious treasure, a jewel of such particularity that for a moment I lost myself and believed her.

For the next ten years—until the building where the lasts were housed burned down—I'd scan magazines with my mother, looking for shoes. I'd send the pictures to Ferragamo's and, for $35 a pair, I'd receive the most amazing creations: olive-green suede with an orange leaf, gray leather with a black heel like an umbrella, my wedding shoes, with seed pearls in the shape of a butterfly. They were not exactly right for a young woman in the shoeless '60s. But they were beautiful.

My mother was a quiet, mysterious woman of understated elegance. When she died, I discovered in her closet shelves of shoes, the price tags still attached. Suddenly I could see her in the shoe department; arthritis had made it impossible for her to wear the slender high heels and strappy sandals she adored. But she would buy them anyway, pretending she was going to a dance.

She believed that anything is possible in life, and that she should always be ready for surprises—a philosophy she had taught me with the full measure of her love. 🕊

Life in These United States

AS A mother of five, I'd like to think my "labors" do not go unappreciated. However, one evening as I was preparing dinner, my 13-year-old son told me about a movie he'd seen in health class of a woman giving birth, and how painful and scary the whole thing looked. Just as I was thinking maybe now he'll have a little more empathy for me, he said, "I feel sorry for Dad having to watch that five times."

Rita Henkel

Letting Go

BY LITTY MATHEW

December 2009/January 2010

THE TABLE turned out to be the hardest to give away. My husband, Melkon, and I had made it when we were dating—our very first woodworking project. Melkon had drawn a high, slim-legged sideboard on the back of a napkin at our favorite sushi joint; I'd added design touches of my own. Together, we'd shopped for streaked poplar the color of honey, chosen hand-painted Mexican tiles for the top, and set up a mini-workshop in the breakfast nook of my suburban Los Angeles apartment.

It had taken us a week to finish the thing, and its

value was more than sentimental: We used it whenever we had company. So I shouldn't have been surprised that Melkon objected—loudly—when I proposed passing it on to someone else.

To be honest, though, I hadn't thought much about how he would react. I was in the middle of an experiment aimed at remaking my relationship with stuff—one that involved parting with some of the objects I cared about most. If my actions seemed selfless, my motives were anything but.

A few months back, I'd fallen into a funk brought on by simultaneous downturns in the national economy, my household income, and, not coincidentally, the joy quotient of my seven-year-old marriage. Vaguely ashamed of my troubles, I kept mum about them. I was feeling cut off from almost everyone I knew, including myself.

Like millions of other Americans, I had come to rely on an all-purpose remedy for the blues—a trip to the mall. But now, when I got home and clipped the price tags off a bagful of blouses, I felt worse than before. In a recession, retail therapy somehow loses its restorative power.

Still, I needed some way to escape the sense of constriction that had settled over my life. So I called my pal Gloria, who's a few degrees more free-spirited than I am, a decade older and several centuries wiser.

"I've got to find a substitute for shopping," I told

her. "I want the high without the credit card hangover. Or the feeling of self-loathing whenever I open my closet."

Gloria suggested I do the *opposite* of shopping. "And I don't mean just giving to Goodwill, honey. You should try holding a Giveaway."

THE GIVEAWAY, or Wopila, is a tradition of the Lakota Sioux, whom Gloria had gotten to know while working as a journalist on the Rosebud Reservation in South Dakota. On important occasions—birthdays, weddings, funerals—the Lakota pass out gifts rather than receive them. Often, they spend months making or collecting items that will be useful or delightful to the recipients.

Gloria's Lakota friends had given her everything from new gym socks to hand-beaded earrings to sheaves of aromatic sage. In turn, she'd become a champion giver, lavishing those close to her with bounty. Gloria's special twist was to give away her own favorite possessions. Over the years, I'd ended up with mosaics she'd crafted by hand, stylish sweaters she'd barely worn, a brand-new pair of boots and a selection of her mother's vintage dresses. For Gloria, no special occasion was necessary. "Hey," she'd say, in her child-of-the-'60s way, "there'll always be new things, so pass on the ones you have." But her motivation was clearly the same as the Lakota's: to strengthen relationships, to revel in the pleasure of generosity, and to keep from feeling that her stuff owned *her*.

As it happened, Gloria wasn't the first person to tell me about the Giveaway. My father had worked on the same reservation, as a doctor; once, before leaving on a long trip, he gave me a rainbow-striped blanket that a Lakota friend had given him as a token of appreciation.

He also pointed out that my own family had a similar tradition. We're the other kind of Indian, with roots in India itself. When my parents were kids there, newlyweds rarely received blenders. Instead, they invited passersby to share in the wedding banquet.

But I grew up mostly in the United States, and I'd never been to Rosebud. I wasn't sure I had what it would take to throw a Giveaway of my own.

I DECIDED to start with something small. Gloria's sister, Marina, a fashion editor in Italy, was bedridden after a stroke. It occurred to me that my favorite earrings—petite gold hoops with tiny diamonds—might help her feel more stylish and would be comfortable to wear while propped on a pillow.

Relinquishing them wasn't easy; it took a week to work up the courage. But finally, I handed them to Gloria while we browsed the sale rack at the Gap. Feeling a bit embarrassed, I didn't mention that I was following her advice. She didn't ask, either, but simply thanked me and went on examining jeans.

Neither of us bought anything, even on sale. Yet I glided out of the store on a cloud of euphoria, as jazzed as I'd ever been after a successful shopping expedition. In the ensuing weeks, whenever I thought of Marina wearing my earrings ("She says they look beautiful on her," Gloria reported), the sensation returned full force. No purchase I'd ever made for myself had ever had such a lasting effect.

Next, I gave a green silk shawl to my friend Judy, a graphic artist who loves lush fabrics, and a heavy copper saucepan to Kaumudi, a caterer friend with a new business. Leaving the post office, I gave a book of stamps to a guy outside the door. I could tell he thought I was running a scam. "Really, it's on me," I insisted. "You don't want to go in there today." When he saw the line, he nodded and shook my hand.

With each Giveaway, I felt lighter, as if the weight of the past months' worries were lifting. Though my finances hadn't improved appreciably, my anxiety level sure had. And I felt a new closeness with my giftees. My sense of isolation was dissolving.

Then I came up with my boldest challenge yet, and perhaps my most foolhardy: to give away the table Melkon and I had made together. The recipient would be his just-married cousin Guillermo. "Let's surprise him, sweetie," I suggested over dinner one evening. Guillermo had always admired the piece, I said, and would be thrilled to own it.

My husband looked at me as if I'd suddenly begun speaking Esperanto. "And where do you suggest we put the food at our next party?"

"We'll work something out."

Until then, Melkon had silently watched my Giveaways, weighing whether they were just an annoying new hobby or a sign of impending mental breakdown. Now I was asking him to participate. I knew it seemed unfair, but something told me that it might be good for both of us.

"But it's the only thing we've made together," he protested.

"That's what will make it so special for Guillermo and Arus."

"It's not even that nice, Litty," Melkon said, rubbing at the tabletop. "The grout is starting to crumble."

"It doesn't matter."

Like most people, Melkon was accustomed to giving away only items he no longer needed—a trash bag of castoffs on the doorstep of a nonprofit, for instance. "Let me think about it," he said.

He thought about it for a week. Actually, we argued about it for a week, in a series of emotional exchanges that touched on other issues we'd been avoiding—the burnout that came from starting up a business together, our frustrations with ourselves, each other and the world. How could each of us grow without leaving the other behind? What could we let go?

By the end, it felt like we had cleared up more than just the pile of clutter that usually accumulated on the table. And Melkon was ready to part with our precious piece of furniture.

We heaved it into the back of our SUV and drove to Guillermo's place. He was waiting outside.

"You're giving us the table?" he cried. "Wow! It'll be the first piece of furniture in our living room!"

Melkon grinned—something I hadn't seen him do for days. "Yeah," he said. "It'll look great in your new house." We were both smiling as we drove home.

Now when we have dinner parties, we lay out the buffet on any handy surface. When someone asks where the table went, Melkon will say, glancing at me from the corner of his eye, "There's this fascinating Lakota tradition called the Giveaway. It involves not having a place for the hors d'oeuvres—and getting to know your wife a little better."

Humor in Uniform

A DISTRAUGHT driver was grateful when our Marine son, Jim, stopped to help put out a fire in her car. "I prayed, 'Please let the next car stop,' and it was you," the woman gushed.

Jim's mother was also pleased when she heard the story.

"Who would have thought," she told him, "that you'd be the answer to any girl's prayers?" *Richard Bell*

She Gave Her Father Life

BY HENRY HURT

November 1996

JEANNE SZUBER groped in the darkness for the telephone beside the bed. The voice was unfamiliar as her eyes found the green numerals of the digital clock: 4:40 in the morning. *Surely a wrong number,* Jeanne thought, as she tried to make sense of what the woman with the polite Southern accent was saying.

"Heavens, no," Jeanne said gruffly, a frown crossing her strong face. "Our daughter does not have a tattoo of a little feather on her foot. What are you talking about?"

The caller, from a hospital emergency room in

Tennessee, explained that a young woman, said by a companion to be Patti Szuber, had been in a car accident. A chill swept over Jeanne Szuber. "Wait a minute," she said, her voice weakening. "Maybe Patti does have a tattoo. She asked me if she could get one and I said no. Maybe she did it anyway. And she is on a camping trip in Tennessee."

There was silence. Jeanne felt her husband, Chester, stirring at her side. Then the woman spoke again: "The girl's in very bad shape."

Jeanne's body tightened as her mind held on to an image of effervescent, bright-eyed Patti, 22 years old, the youngest of their six children and one of only two still living at home. She managed to squeeze barely audible words from her throat: "How bad?"

"I'm so sorry," the voice in the night said gently. "I have to tell you that death may be moments away. I'm so very sorry."

Jeanne looked at her husband of 37 years. "It's Patti," she whispered, though she knew that Chet knew. "They don't think there's a chance."

Chester Szuber went to the kitchen, where he picked up the phone and sought more details from the hospital in Knoxville, 500 miles away from the Szuber home outside of Detroit. He learned that Patti had sustained a traumatic head injury when the car she was riding in crashed on a curving road in Great Smoky Mountains National Park.

An empty misery settled over him. The greatest joy in Chet's life was his big, close-knit family. He and Jeanne cherished the sight of their four sons and two daughters prospering and starting their own families. Though Chet would never pick a favorite child, everyone knew that, to him, Patti was very special. Her high spirits and exuberance had always charmed him.

From the earliest days, Chet and Patti were so close that the Szuber children liked to joke: "If you really want something from Dad, put your hands on your hips like Patti and bat your eyes." The jest was based on a good measure of reality, but no one seems to have resented it.

As dawn broke on that August 18, 1994, Jeanne and Chet sat looking at each other—numb, glassy-eyed, saying little, waiting for their children to arrive so they could decide what to do. Patti's elderly gray and white cat, confused by the break in routine, prowled about the kitchen. She had been "rescued" 11 years earlier from what 12-year-old Patti insisted would be a miserable life without the Szuber family. To Patti, the cat was one of the most beautiful creatures she had ever seen. And she had given it the most elegant name she could think of: Ashley Marlene. Where the name came from, no one knew.

"Am I dreaming?" Chet said to Jeanne, as Ashley Marlene, in the loaf position on the kitchen floor, looked up at them. "Is any of this really happening to us?"

JEANNE SZUBER cradled the newborn baby, rocking her and smiling as she studied the funny little face. "Patricia Jeanne" was the name they'd chosen for her.

"She was the most beautiful baby," Chet says. "She was so pink and good-natured, and she just kept getting prettier and sweeter for the rest of her life."

Jeanne and Chet took little Patti home to Berkley, a suburban town next-door to Detroit. Located on tree-lined Phillips Street, the Szuber house is one of hundreds of small, well-kept homes in a neighborhood where families have known each other for generations. Jeanne Szuber grew up a block away. She speaks with affection for her neighborhood—and notes with pride that the Szuber house and the three next to it have produced 20 children.

"The church told us to have all these kids but then didn't tell us what to do with them!" Jeanne says, laughing. But it was this bounty of children—and the powerful love for them—that made the neighborhood the perfect place for Patti Szuber, her four brothers and her sister.

Chet and Jeanne were happy in their early years, but they also lived with a chilling concern. Something was wrong with Chet's heart.

For their first ten years, Chet never had a signal

that he wasn't completely fit. Six feet tall and 160 pounds, he loved to play center field on a team in a men's baseball league. But when he turned 32, all of that began to change. While jogging one day, Chet's heart went crazy—"thumping and racing like it would jump out of my chest." Doctors disagreed about what was wrong. Some even insisted that they could detect no symptoms of heart trouble.

But the terrifying spells became a regular part of Chet's life. Finally, after one particularly painful week, a battery of sophisticated tests led to a devastating diagnosis: Chet had suffered a heart attack. "Mr. Szuber," the doctor told him, "you have the heart of a 70-year-old."

The doctor explained that due to advanced arteriosclerosis, Chet's arteries, including those immediately around his heart, were clogged with plaque—hardened far beyond anything to be expected in a man in his 30s. The result was myriad occlusions in the arteries, leading to a heart attack.

"But how is this possible?" Chet countered, citing his healthful life-style and his seemingly good physical condition. "My grandparents on both sides lived into their nineties."

Then Chet remembered something he usually tried to push out of his mind: his mother—perfectly healthy as far as her family could see—had died suddenly of a heart attack at the age of 56.

"You may have inherited your mother's heart," the doctor said. "Whatever the cause, the point is, your heart is in bad shape." In those days, nearly 25 years ago, few of today's medical options were available to help a man in Chet's condition.

At 37, four months after his heart attack, Chet underwent his first surgery. Over the next 20 years, he experienced many more heart attacks and five more surgical procedures.

Three times—in 1973, 1982 and 1987—Chet had major bypass surgery just to replace clogged arteries around his heart. During the last operation, he was walloped by a massive heart attack while he was still on the operating table. It was miraculous that he ever woke up.

Patti's birth in 1971, just a year before her father's first major heart attack, coincided with Chet's realization that he had a lousy heart and that he had better enjoy his children while he could. The youngest Szuber child by five years, Patti also took her place as the youngest among the Szubers' neighborhood friends.

From her first days, she was cuddled by just about anyone who came along. The other Szuber children competed to see who would get to hold her and feed her and put her to bed. Out of this arose a confidence that made Patti quite certain she was welcome anywhere—and a generosity that made her want to share the warmth and caring others had lavished on her.

When she was still tiny, she used to ride off on her tricycle to make visits around the neighborhood. While attending Pattengill Elementary School a few blocks away, it became her habit to walk home at lunch time with a friend in tow, often a child who was new to the area or feeling a little lonely.

Patti was a child who was full of affection and high spirits. She was always laughing and talking—hands moving, face smiling.

To Jeanne, one of Patti's most endearing features was that she loved to lean against her mother. Standing or sitting, Jeanne would soon enough notice that Patti—as a toddler and later as a teen-ager—was leaning on her, giving her small hugs.

In another sense, Patti also leaned on her no-nonsense, businesslike father. The son of Polish immigrant farmers in northern Michigan, Chet grew up working on the family farm in the late '40s. He dreamed of going to law school, but in college that dream disappeared when he met Jeanne Wood. Soon they were married.

An extremely articulate man with a heavy, squarely built face, Chet found himself well-suited to work as a salesman, and for 16 years he sold home appliances and supplies for Sears. To make extra money at Christmastime for his rapidly growing family, he began trucking in Christmas trees from Canada and selling them at Detroit's sprawling open-air

Eastern Market. Soon enough, the whole family was involved—even Patti, the littlest, who worked decorating wreaths.

In those early days Chet's heart was steadily deteriorating. In 1980 he gave up his Sears job for good. His health made it impossible to continue, and he had to stay at home. By then, Patti was eight years old. Because of his illness, Chet and his daughter spent even more time together.

And nowhere did Patti and her dad enjoy each other more than during Christmastime at the Eastern Market, an Old World extravaganza where hundreds of vendors gathered throughout the year to offer every imaginable product—from fresh and smoked meats and garden produce to live chickens, ducks and rabbits. Fresh fish from the Great Lakes were displayed in large beds of shaved ice. Baked and home-canned goods, as well as all sorts of trinkets and home accessories, were for sale everywhere.

All through the usually frigid Decembers, Chet and his children sold their trees and wreaths. Like the other sellers, Chet hoped for bitterly cold weather. It helped the customers make up their minds more quickly, he always said. Patti loved the carnival atmosphere of the market—the Christmas music, hot chocolate and foods such as roasted nuts, pretzels and steaming sausages. And she loved tagging along with her father.

On Christmas Eve, when the tree selling was finally over, Chet was so tired that he fell into bed. But for Patti the excitement was just beginning. She had made sure that the Szuber Christmas tree was picked early, and she had a big say in how it was decorated.

Paul Pelto, one of the Szubers' closest friends, still remembers one Christmas Eve vividly. He arrived at the Szubers' dressed as a jolly Santa Claus, bringing gifts for the children. Standing back in awe at who was in her living room, little Patti—about four at the time—kept staring at him, smiling shyly. Pelto began to wonder if she suspected who he really was.

"Then," he says, "she grabbed her favorite doll and ran over and handed it to me, like she wanted to give a gift to Santa before he gave one to her. That's the kind of little kid she was."

THERE WAS also a strong, feisty side to Patti. She refused to tolerate prejudice, fiercely defended the underdog and, above all, loved lost creatures such as the homely Ashley Marlene. This instinct became the source of many disputes between Patti and her father.

One of their biggest disagreements was about Patti's friendship with an erratic free spirit named Todd Herbst—a neighborhood boy Chet viewed as "a major nuisance." From Chet's standpoint Todd constantly had big plans but never delivered. As Chet would say to Patti, "That kid's all show and no go."

Chet saw Todd as a shiftless young man who paraded about in outlandish clothes and wore hairstyles calculated to outrage normal people like himself.

But Todd and Patti had known each other since fifth grade. They rode bikes together, went camping and played pinball at Van Dyke Sports Center. They liked to hang out and talk at the local graveyard—always sitting on the big stone near the middle marked with the name "Gilbert."

The two grew up together, and when they were older, they maintained their bond. They enjoyed going dancing or having dinner at one of the fancy restaurants where Todd worked as a waiter.

In spite of Patti's close friendship with Todd, Chet worried that Todd was a bad influence on his daughter. Jeanne, however, argued that Todd was another person Patti felt needed her help—like the lonely children she used to bring home from school. But Chet remained unconvinced.

What made matters worse was that Todd was at the Szubers' house often—with his hair dyed green and, later, orange. Whenever Todd would appear at the door, Chet would look through the young man and call out, "Patti, your friend is here."

Chester Szuber was at least grateful that Todd and Patti had no romantic interest in each other. In fact Patti had plenty of regular boyfriends, but they never interfered with her durable, uncomplicated friendship with Todd Herbst—whatever the color of his hair.

Patti once explained their friendship to her mother: "When you tell a girl something, she blabs it. But I can count on Todd. He is totally trustworthy. Who could have a better friend?"

After high school—motivated by her father's precarious health—Patti went on to college to study nursing, planning to become an operating-room technician. In her spare time she earned money interning with a doctor and, later, working as a front-desk clerk at a local hotel.

As for Todd, he continued to wait on tables in restaurants, taking pride in the fact that the restaurants that would hire him were increasingly fancy.

Whatever he and Patti were doing, their friendship remained as steady as before.

Two decades after he began selling Christmas trees, Chet, with the help of his family, began turning their 400 acres in northern Michigan, where he had grown up, into a tree farm. It was Chet who plotted the growth of the trees and the development of the business. Although it was a long process, by the early '90s he was selling thousands of his own trees each year at the Eastern Market. But by then he was so debilitated he could get around the farm for only a few hours a day.

At home it was hard for him to get out of bed, and it exhausted him to move across a room. His sons and friends had to help him into the woods to sit in a deer blind during the hunting season.

By nature an energetic, take-charge man, Chet now lived in a quagmire of pain and lethargy. At 58, his life was all but over. The only thing the family could do was pray. Further bypass surgery was too risky. For the previous four years, Chet had been on a waiting list for a heart transplant. With each passing week he descended a little further into a misery made worse by his awful realization that a healthy person had to die in order for him to live.

One night, during these dark days, Todd Herbst paid one of his frequent visits, making his way past a glowering Chet to see Patti. As the boy and girl played cards and watched television late into the night, a show came on in which some people were killed in an automobile accident.

"If I ever got killed," Patti declared, "I'd really want my father to have my heart." This was something she had expressed many times to Todd.

But on this occasion, Todd said to Patti: "But I bet if I got killed and they offered your dad my heart, he wouldn't take it!"

"He probably wouldn't," Patti said, chuckling over the continuing saga of her father and her friend.

WITHIN HOURS of the early-morning telephone call from the hospital, the Szuber family—plus a dozen close friends and relatives—were heading to Knoxville to be at Patti's bedside. Over and over, Jeanne and Chet told people how they had spoken to Patti just a few hours before the accident. Over and over, they replayed the events that had culminated in this living nightmare.

As a last fling before she returned to the academic grind of nursing school, she and Todd Herbst had set out for a camping trip in the Great Smoky Mountains. The August weather in the mountains was magnificent. The mist hanging in the hollows, drifting upward, enchanted Patti and Todd.

The two friends made camp in Kentucky the first night and reached Tennessee on the second day. In Gatlinburg, Patti and Todd paid $20 for a helicopter ride up into the mountains. Looking down, they could see the hollows and peaks softened by the summer haze that gives the Smokies their name. The helicopter ride—Patti's first—was so thrilling that, back on the ground, she telephoned her parents to tell them how much fun she was having.

After setting up camp, she and Todd had supper and, later that evening, found a roadside tavern called What's Up?—a place filled with music and local people their age. They then joined new-found friends at a party nearby. "We had such a great time dancing and drinking beer," Todd says today. "But we talked about how one of us had to drive, so I stopped drinking an hour and a half before we left. We were always careful about that . . ."

Their good intentions were undone by alcohol and speed. The crash occurred at 2:20 a.m. on a sharp curve in the mountains near Pigeon Forge. Traveling 20 miles an hour over the speed limit, Todd lost control and hit a rock outcropping. According to police, the car skidded 832 feet. The vehicle flipped and rolled, then rolled again and again. Neither Patti nor Todd was wearing a seat belt.

When the car came to rest, Patti had been thrown out and lay on her back unconscious, blood pouring from the back of her head. A swatch of her hair was found on the pavement 60 feet away. Todd had numerous cuts and bruises but no serious injuries.

Paramedics, alerted by motorists, soon arrived. Shortly after that, a rescue helicopter clattered down to take Patti to the University of Tennessee Medical Center in Knoxville, 15 minutes away.

Todd's blood-alcohol level was .14, notably higher than Tennessee's .10 mark for legal intoxication. He was led away by the police to be treated for his cuts and later was charged with several violations, including drunken driving. Jailed overnight, Todd was released the next morning. He got a policeman to drive him to Knoxville, 45 miles away, so he could check on Patti. He was sure she would be fine.

But at the hospital Todd learned the brutal truth—

that Patti had suffered severe brain damage and was being kept alive by machines. He also learned that Jeanne and Chester Szuber—as well as numerous family members, friends and neighbors, including his own parents—were on their way to Tennessee.

"There are no words for the horror I felt," Todd says. "The best friend I had in the whole world was in the next room dying, and I was responsible. I was petrified to think of facing Mr. Szuber." Throughout the day, as he waited for others to arrive, Todd went in to see Patti. He sat beside her bed crying and holding her hand.

One of the first friends to arrive, after driving all night from Detroit, was Thom Bishop. Patti had been his girlfriend for several years. From the Berkley area, Thom had also known Todd Herbst for years. He saw Todd as a harmless, if aimless, person—someone Patti was extremely close to and was trying to help.

"When I saw Todd standing there," says Thom, "I had to slow down and get my thoughts together. I loved Patti. I really didn't know whether I was going to hit him or hug him. I knew some people who would have felt like killing Todd at that moment."

As Thom approached where Patti lay, he instinctively reached for Todd and embraced him, and the two young men wept.

Later, after Todd took a walk to clear his head, he returned to Patti's room and came face to face with

Jeanne and Chester Szuber. He didn't know if it would be better to vanish or to stay and weather Chet's wrath. Nearly paralyzed with fear, Todd stood, speechless, as they turned toward him.

"As soon as they saw me, Jeanne threw her arms around me and said she loved me," Todd says. Jeanne had always liked Todd and thought Patti was a good influence on him. A moment later Chet embraced him warmly, saying that he knew Todd would never do anything purposely to hurt Patti. All Todd could do was weep with miserable relief.

Then Jeanne and Chester Szuber went into the room to say farewell, forever, to their daughter. The doctors told them Patti's brain was so badly damaged that there was no hope for her life. Lips trembling, Chet leaned down and kissed Patti's cool, soft cheek. Tears ran down his face as he held one of her hands in both of his. Jeanne stood on the opposite side of the bed, holding the other hand as she brushed her fingers through her daughter's hair. Except for some swelling and a bruise over her left eye, Patti looked as if she were asleep.

Jeanne and Chet could see the green monitors alive with squiggly lines showing strong activity in their daughter's heart. Twitches in her body and movement in one of her legs stirred their hope that at any moment their precious child would suddenly wake up and be fine.

But that was not to happen.

CHESTER SZUBER'S thick hand moved the pen deliberately across the blank spaces on the forms that lay on the coffee table in front of him. His lips quivered as he signed his name, giving permission for his daughter's organs and tissues to be removed and transplanted into other people whose lives would be renewed. He knew this was Patti's wish. When she was 18, she had signed an organ donor card and ever since had urged others to do the same.

Standing by during these grim moments were Patti's mother, her brothers and sister, and the priest who had administered the last rites. She had been declared brain dead at 11:35 that Sunday morning, three days after the accident. Now machines would keep Patti's body functioning until her organs were removed.

Guiding Jeanne and Chet through this painful process was Susan Fredenberg, a nurse with Tennessee Donor Services. A gentle woman in her early 30s, she works to establish rapport with a donor family and make arrangements for placing the organs.

The evening before Patti was declared dead, Susan had suggested to Chet that legally he could be the recipient of Patti's heart. He rejected the idea so quickly that Susan was convinced he probably never thought about what she was saying—if he had heard her words at all.

Now, with Patti officially declared dead and the donation forms signed, Susan Fredenberg returned to the subject: "Mr. Szuber, we need to talk about Patti's heart. It is possible it could go to you—for you to have it transplanted."

Chet still did not grasp what this woman was saying. He was consumed with the immediate problems of planning a funeral and getting Patti's body and the rest of the family back to Michigan. He shook his head, thinking, *What on earth is she talking about?*

Then, as her words took hold, Chet was shocked. The idea had never remotely occurred to him. If he were to accept the offer, he would be reminded of Patti's death with every beat of her heart. Far better, he thought, to be dead himself.

He stared at Susan Fredenberg. "Absolutely not!" Chet said almost fiercely. "The answer is no. Never!"

"Mr. Szuber," Susan Fredenberg said gently, "Patti cannot live. But maybe you can."

Tears sprang to Chet's eyes as he said once more, "Absolutely not."

Susan Fredenberg quickly withdrew. She spent the next hour stabilizing Patti's body and checking with the organ donation network to locate recipients for Patti's organs.

Back in the small room the hospital had provided the Szubers, Chet lay down on the bed and closed his eyes. Never had he been assaulted by so many emotions. He willed his mind back to planning Patti's funeral.

As he lay there alone, a thought came to him: *Is it possible that Patti would want me to have her heart? Is it possible I really would not be taking her heart so much as she would be giving it to me?* Chet got up from the bed and walked outside the room to a small patio where his wife and one of the children sat talking. He asked Jeanne to come into the room.

"How would you feel if I had Patti's heart?" he asked almost brusquely.

Jeanne was stunned by the shift in Chet's position—and frightened at the idea that her husband might not survive the risky procedure. "No, we can't do that," she said. "I just lost Patti, and I'm not going to lose you too. And how can we have Patti's funeral if you're in the hospital?"

Just the idea brought her to tears. But she felt she should find out what their children had to say. She went back to the patio and sat down just a few feet from his window.

From inside the room Chet could hear the voices of his sons who had come by to say farewell to their parents before they caught a plane back to Michigan. Suddenly it was quiet as Jeanne spoke to them all. "They've offered your dad Patti's heart," she said softly. "What do you think?"

At first there was silence, and then Chet heard his children's voices rise together in a tone of affirmation—the words unclear but the message unmistakable. Finally Jeanne said solemnly, "Go see your dad."

Moments later Chet's room was filled with his children. One by one, each told him that this was exactly what Patti would want—that nothing would have meant more to her than for her father to have her heart.

Within minutes they had sent for Susan Fredenberg. Gathering his strength and once again taking charge, Chet turned to Susan and his family and spoke with firm dignity: "It would be a joy to have Patti's heart."

DR. JEFFREY Altshuler, on vacation, was leaving his house near Detroit about 4:30 that Sunday afternoon, on his way to a hockey rink where he intended to spend several hours on the ice pursuing his great passion. A phone call stopped him at the door. As a surgeon who had performed 70 heart transplants in his career, Altshuler was accustomed to having his vacations interrupted.

Over the next few minutes, an extraordinary story unfolded. Transplant coordinator Caroline Medcoff told Altshuler that the daughter of their patient, Chester Szuber, lay brain dead in a Knoxville hospital, her heart still beating strongly. Initial tests indicated that the match could work.

The immediate question was whether to do the

transplant in Tennessee or Michigan. Tennessee made the most sense logistically, but ultimately it was not feasible to make the needed arrangements on a speedy basis. Moreover the Szuber family insisted that the operation take place in Michigan, so at least all but Chet could attend Patti's funeral.

The paramount question to be resolved was whether Patti's heart would work for her father. Dr. Altshuler could not decide that until he held Patti's heart in his own hands and examined it. But what he did know was that never to his knowledge had a child's heart been transplanted into a parent.

One of the Altshuler team's first calls was to Max Freeman, a General Motors engineer who is also a co-owner of a corporate flight service. He and Altshuler had become friends over the years, and when asked, Freeman often flew transplant teams to recover organs.

"We'll take off around one in the morning," Dr. Altshuler told Freeman. The surgeon instructed his organ recovery team to assemble at the hospital at midnight for a briefing. Timing would be critical, for no more than four hours should pass from the time a heart is stopped and removed from a donor until the moment it begins beating in the recipient's chest.

At the same time that Altshuler would be traveling 1000 miles to recover Patti's heart, his surgical partner, Dr. Francis L. Shannon, would wait at William

Beaumont Hospital in Royal Oak, just outside of Detroit, to make sure Chet was ready for implantation as soon as the heart arrived.

Meanwhile, Jeanne and Chet had flown from Knoxville and arrived at the hospital just after midnight. They were alone in Chet's room as they awaited Dr. Altshuler. "We just have to keep remembering one thing," Chet said to Jeanne. "This is what Patti would want."

"There's something else," Jeanne said, thinking about their 37 years of marriage and the fact that this might be their last moment together on earth. "I know we've always loved each other, but I'm sorry we haven't said it more often." Chet put his arms around her.

Dr. Altshuler, a friendly, easy-going man in his 40s with a shock of black hair, strode into the room. This would be the last chance he and Chet would have to talk before surgery, and Altshuler wanted to be sure his patient understood the risks and was at peace with the unusual emotional stress facing him.

He explained the whole procedure: he would fly to Knoxville, remove Patti's heart and bring it back to this hospital. Dr. Altshuler was ultimately convinced that Chet could handle the special trauma—a conclusion he based on his nearly four years of working with him as a patient. "I knew that Mr. Szuber thinks things through, and I felt comfortable that once he reached his decision in this case, it was the right one."

As Altshuler was leaving, Chet called to him. He was thinking of Patti, and with his voice breaking, he made one final request.

"Please," he said. "Be gentle."

"Lifeguard flight," Max Freeman announced to the tower as the sleek white Cessna Citation sped toward the runway at 1:20 that Monday morning. To air-traffic controllers the "Lifeguard" designation is the same as flashing lights and a siren are to highway traffic—giving that flight top priority for takeoff and landing over almost everything else. It also qualifies for the best routes to Knoxville.

Instantly cleared, the little jet rose sharply into the night air, streaking over Detroit and heading on a southerly course for eastern Tennessee. Soon it was cruising at 400 miles per hour at an altitude of 37,000 feet.

In the cabin Dr. Altshuler and three members of his team sat quietly. Lynn Flores, the team perfusionist, had been on other transplant trips with Dr. Altshuler, but never one like this. "It's always both sad and thrilling, but this was different. I found myself thinking about myself and my own children."

Flores's job was to administer the chemicals that bring the beating heart to a complete stop. Only then can it be removed and packed in ice. From the instant she stops the heart, the clock begins ticking until the organ is restarted in the recipient's chest. Four hours is the optimum limit for a heart to be at rest. On the floor behind Flores lay her bag of chemicals and instruments—as well as a small red and white Igloo ice chest.

The plane touched down in Knoxville at 2:50 a.m. and taxied to a small corporate hangar. The team got into an ambulance, leaving Max Freeman and his co-pilot ready and waiting at the plane.

At the hospital Patti's chest was already open when the team arrived, the beating heart displayed. Even though brain dead, the donor patient is treated at every step as if she were actually alive. Indeed on some levels it appears that she is—with the ventilator and heart monitor flashing and beeping as they track functioning organs.

Dr. Altshuler spent a few minutes examining Patti's heart, checking to see if it had any bruises from the accident that might cause complications. When he was convinced the heart was sound, Lynn Flores released the chemicals into the aorta, flooding the heart with potassium cardioplegia.

Patti's heart beat for the last time at 3:56 a.m. The lines on the monitors became straight; the small beeps ceased. A calm settled over the room.

"We keep our emotions to ourselves," says Lynn Flores. "But at that moment I always say a prayer, and that night I said one for Patti."

At that point Dr. Altshuler removed Patti's heart. After a final inspection he packed it in the cooler. He then went to a telephone and called his partner in Michigan to get Chester Szuber ready. His daughter's heart was on the way.

AT THE Knoxville airfield in the dead of night, pilot Max Freeman was deep in thought as he awaited the return of the Altshuler team. He saw another small jet, a Lifeguard flight, quickly ease into place at the corporate hangar and let off another transplant team. Sometimes Freeman has seen as many as four jets converge and then rush skyward into the night in different directions, bearing a person's most precious gifts.

In Patti's case her organs left Knoxville that night and took with them the hope of vision to two people, kidneys to two others, a liver to a 15-year-old girl— and her heart to her father.

"It's during that wait that you have time to think," Freeman says. "All the technology at work in a mission like this is humbling: the surgeons, the skilled technicians, the equipment to keep the donor's organs going. It really is the ultimate coming together of human skills. And then you have an airplane whose speed makes the difference in whether or not it all works."

By 4:25 a.m. Dr. Altshuler and his team were back on board. Freeman accelerated down the runway, and the Cessna soared into the hot Tennessee night—speeding toward Detroit where surgeons were already opening Chester Szuber's chest. The team was tense because of the close timing. The Igloo ice chest was on the floor beside Lynn Flores. Fighting strong head winds all the way, Freeman knew every minute counted.

Morning had broken when the jet touched down at 6:10 at Detroit Metro Airport. Waiting beside the corporate hangar was a green and white Bell LongRanger helicopter, ready to relay the team and the heart to Beaumont Hospital. The team quickly boarded, and 15 minutes later the LongRanger settled onto Beaumont's helipad.

By the time Dr. Altshuler walked into the operating room, Chet's chest had been cut open, and a heart-lung machine was standing by to keep him alive. Ignoring his fatigue, Dr. Altshuler immediately removed the old heart and began to stitch Patti's heart into her father's chest.

Finally, his work done, Dr. Altshuler released the clamps and sent Chet's blood from the heart-lung machine into the new heart. It is only at that moment that anyone knows whether or not the new heart will work. And to add to the team's concern, Patti's heart had been at rest almost two hours over the four-hour mark.

Instantly at 9:47 a.m. Patti's heart sprang to life, pumping blood through her father's body with a power he had not felt for a quarter of a century. Unlike a repaired heart, which can take months to reach full potential, a healthy transplanted heart almost always reaches its potential immediately.

When Chet eased toward consciousness a little past noon that day, one of his first impressions was the clarity of his mind. After his earlier surgeries, grogginess and confusion and pain tormented him as he tried to gain control, to assess his condition.

But this time his sensations were completely different: "I knew my memory had deteriorated, but I didn't realize what a fog I had been in until I started to wake up that day. My mind was working like a kid's. I knew exactly what was going on and that things had gone well." Even the lingering pain from his horrendous surgery was light.

When Jeanne went in to see her husband that afternoon, her emotions were as raw as an open wound. All she could think of was that Patti's body was in Tennessee, but her daughter's heart was beating right here in Chet's chest.

What Jeanne beheld was beyond anything she ever dreamed possible. "Chet's face was pink instead of the usual gray," Jeanne says, still barely holding her emotions. "His lips weren't white anymore but pink. And his eyes were clear and bright—like Patti's."

Within a few hours, Chet was sitting on the side of his bed. The next day he was on his feet, able to take a few steps. As the doctors predicted, Chet's emotions were on a roller-coaster ride—ranging from exhilaration to grief as he thought of his daughter.

A few days later the family gathered in Berkley at Our Lady of LaSalette Church for Patti's funeral. Chet rested in his hospital room, along with a few close friends. One of them was Paul Pelto, the Santa Claus to whom four-year-old Patti had offered her favorite doll. As Paul looked at the newly transformed Chet, he remembered Patti's instinct for giving—an instinct that, as it turned out, ran as deep as life itself.

FOR MORE than two years now, Patti's heart has given her father a fresh life he could never have imagined. He has an energy that allows him to do things his illness had once made impossible, including hunting caribou in the freezing weather of the subarctic. Chet's tree farm is thriving as never before.

The principal person at the Szubers' farm is their son Bob. For him the defining moment of his sister's gift to their father came at the end of a long summer day in which he saw Chet doing more work than he had in years. "When I saw Dad driving home on a tractor, smiling, with a grandkid on each knee, that's when it all came together for me. Patti would be so thrilled."

Chet thinks about Patti all the time—almost as if she's a constant companion. He is in regular touch with his physician at Beaumont Hospital and does what the doctor tells him to do. "I'm not only taking care of myself, I'm taking care of Patti too."

When Chet's not working on the farm, he travels the country telling the story of his daughter's gifts of life and pleading with people to understand the importance of her example.

"Patti may be gone," says Jeanne, "but she's not dead. She lives on in so many others. Any one of us can make the same gifts, and we should."

"What's happened here," adds Chet, "is the greatest miracle this side of heaven. Sometimes people's lifework doesn't begin until after they die."

Occasionally Chet even feels that having Patti's heart gives him some of her feelings as well. When urged to bring a wrongful-death lawsuit against Todd Herbst, Chet refused. When Todd was charged with involuntary manslaughter under federal law—since the accident took place in a national park—Chet appealed to the judge for leniency, pleading that the young man had been punished enough by losing his best friend. (Todd was sentenced to one year in a prison work camp. He was released this past summer and is now on probation for another year.)

On the first day of last spring, with snow still swirling in the air, Chester and Jeanne Szuber visit the graveyard where Patti rests, the same one where Patti and Todd used to meet to talk at the old Gilbert marker. It is only a few blocks from the Szubers' house.

At Patti's marker Jeanne and Chet tidy up little sticks and leaves blown there by the March wind. Chet gestures toward the words engraved on the stone, his fingers almost touching the inscription: "The Happiest Angel in Heaven."

"Do you think she really is?" he's asked.

Chet's strong face crumples a little and his jaw tightens. "I hope so," he says quietly.

It is a hope well founded. In going through papers after Patti's death, Jeanne came across a bright card filled with hearts that Patti had given Chet on Father's Day, 1992. On it she had written a prayer and a promise:

"I'm very proud of your strength and courage. Things will work out, and you will be as good as new soon.

"With love, always, Patti." 🦢

Quotable Quotes

IF YOU'RE lucky enough to do well, it's your responsibility to send the elevator back down.   *Quoted by Kevin Spacey*

• • •

JOY IS one of the only emotions you can't contrive.   *Bono*

Holiday
Holidays
Holiday
Holidays

A Family for Freddie

BY ABBIE BLAIR

December 1964

I REMEMBER THE first time I saw Freddie. He was standing in his playpen at the adoption agency where I work. He gave me a toothy grin. "What a beautiful baby," I thought.

His boarding mother gathered him into her arms. "Will you be able to find a family for Freddie?" she asked.

Then I saw it. Freddie had been born without arms.

"He's so smart. He's only ten months old, and already he walks and talks." She kissed him. "Say 'book' for Mrs. Blair."

Freddie grinned at me and hid his head on his boarding mother's shoulder. "Now, Freddie, don't act that way," she said. "He's really very friendly," she added. "Such a good, good boy."

Freddie reminded me of my own son when he was that age, the same thick dark curls, the same brown eyes.

"You won't forget him, Mrs. Blair? You will try?"

"I won't forget."

I went upstairs and got out my latest copy of the Hard-to-Place list.

> Freddie is a ten-month-old white Protestant boy of English and French background. He has brown eyes, dark-brown hair and fair skin. Freddie was born without arms, but is otherwise in good health. His boarding mother feels he is showing signs of superior mentality, and he is already walking and saying a few words. Freddie is a warm, affectionate child who has been surrendered by his natural mother and is ready for adoption.

"He's ready," I thought. "But who is ready for him?"

It was ten o'clock of a lovely late-summer morning, and the agency was full of couples—couples having interviews, couples meeting babies, families being born. These couples nearly always have the same dream: they want a child as much like themselves as possible, as young as possible and—most important— a child with no medical problem.

"If he develops a problem after we get him," they say, "that is a risk we'll take, just like any other parents. But to pick a baby who already has a problem—that's too much."

And who can blame them?

I wasn't alone in looking for parents for Freddie. Any of the caseworkers meeting a new couple started with a hope: maybe they were for Freddie. But summer slipped into fall, and Freddie was with us for his first birthday party.

"Freddie is so-o-o big," said his boarding mother, stretching out her arms.

"So-o-o big," said Freddie, laughing. "So-o-o big."

And then I found them.

It started out as it always does—an impersonal record in my box, a new case, a new "Home Study," two people who wanted a child. They were Frances and Edwin Pearson. She was 41. He was 45. She was a housewife. He was a truck driver.

I went to see them. They lived in a tiny white frame house in a big yard full of sun and old trees. They greeted me together at the door, eager and scared to death.

Mrs. Pearson produced steaming coffee and oven-warm cookies. They sat before me on the sofa, close together, holding hands. After a moment Mrs. Pearson began: "Today is our wedding anniversary. Eighteen years."

"Good years." Mr. Pearson looked at his wife. "Except—"

"Yes," she said. "Except. Always the 'except.'" She looked around the immaculate room. "It's too neat," she said. "You know?"

I thought of my own living room with my three children. Teenagers now. "Yes," I said. "I know."

"Perhaps we're too old?"

I smiled. "You don't think so," I said. "We don't either."

"You always think it will be this month, and then next month," Mr. Pearson said. "Even when you begin to guess the truth, you don't want to accept it."

"We've tried everything," Mrs. Pearson said. "Examinations. Tests. All kinds of things. Over and over. But nothing ever happened. You just go on hoping and hoping, and time keeps slipping by."

"We've tried to adopt before this," Mr. Pearson said. "One agency told us our apartment was too small, so we got this house. Then another one said I didn't make enough money. We had decided that was it, but this friend told us about you and we decided to make one last try."

"I'm glad," I said.

Mrs. Pearson glanced at her husband proudly. "Can we choose at all?" she asked. "A boy for my husband?"

"We'll try for a boy," I said. "What kind of boy?"

Mrs. Pearson laughed. "How many kinds are

there? Just a boy. My husband is very athletic. He played football in high school; basketball, too, and track. He would be good for a boy."

Mr. Pearson looked at me. "I know you can't tell exactly," he said, "but can you give us any idea how soon? We've waited so long."

I hesitated. There is always this question.

"Next summer maybe," said Mrs. Pearson. "We could take him to the beach."

"That long?" Mr. Pearson said. "Don't you have anyone at all? There *must* be a little boy somewhere.

"Of course," he went on after a pause, "we can't give him as much as other people. We haven't a lot of money saved up."

"We've got a lot of love," his wife said. "We've saved up a lot of that."

"Well," I said cautiously, "there *is* a little boy. He is 13 months old."

"Oh," Mrs. Pearson said, "just a beautiful age."

"I have a picture of him," I said, reaching for my purse. I handed them Freddie's picture.

"He is a wonderful little boy," I said. "But he was born without arms."

They studied the picture in silence. He looked at her. "What do you think, Fran?"

"Kickball," Mrs. Pearson said. "You could teach him kickball."

"Athletics are not so important," Mr. Pearson said.

"He can learn to use his head. Arms he can do without. A head, never. He can go to college. We'll save for it."

"A boy is a boy," Mrs. Pearson insisted. "He needs to play. You can teach him."

"I'll teach him. Arms aren't everything. Maybe we can get him some."

They had forgotten me. But maybe Mr. Pearson was right, I thought. Maybe sometime Freddie could be fitted with artificial arms. He did have nubs where arms should be.

"Then you might like to see him?"

They looked up. "When could we have him?"

"You think you might want him?"

Mrs. Pearson looked at me. "Might?" she said. "*Might?*"

"We want him," her husband said.

Mrs. Pearson went back to the picture. "You've been waiting for us," she said. "Haven't you?"

"His name is Freddie," I said, "but you can change it."

"No," said Mr. Pearson. "Frederick Pearson—it's good together."

And that was it.

There were formalities, of course; and by the time we set the day Christmas lights were strung across city streets and wreaths were hung everywhere.

I met the Pearsons in the waiting room. There was a little snow on them both.

"Your son's here already," I told them. "Let's go upstairs, and I'll bring him to you."

"I've got butterflies," Mrs. Pearson announced. "Suppose he doesn't like us?"

I put my hand on her arm. "I'll get him," I said.

Freddie's boarding mother had dressed him in a new white suit, with a sprig of green holly and red berries embroidered on the collar. His hair shone, a mop of dark curls.

"Going home," Freddie said to me, smiling, as his boarding mother put him in my arms.

"I told him that," she said. "I told him he was going to his new home."

She kissed him, and her eyes were wet.

"Good-bye, dear. Be a good boy."

"Good boy," said Freddie cheerfully. "Going home."

I carried him upstairs to the little room where the Pearsons were waiting. When I got there, I put him on his feet and opened the door.

"Merry Christmas," I said.

Freddie stood uncertainly, rocking a little, gazing intently at the two people before him.

They drank him in.

Mr. Pearson knelt on one knee. "Freddie," he said, "come here. Come to Daddy."

Freddie looked back at me for a moment. Then, turning, he walked slowly toward them; and they reached out their arms and gathered him in. 🦢

A String of Blue Beads

BY FULTON OURSLER

December 1951

PETE RICHARDS was the loneliest man in town on the day Jean Grace opened his door. You may have seen something in the newspapers about the incident at the time it happened, although neither his name nor hers was published, nor was the full story told as I tell it here.

Pete's shop had come down to him from his grandfather. The little front window was strewn with a disarray of old-fashioned things: bracelets and lockets worn in days before the Civil War, gold rings and silver boxes, images of jade and ivory, porcelain figurines.

On this winter's afternoon a child was standing there, her forehead against the glass, earnest and enormous eyes studying each discarded treasure, as if she were looking for something quite special. Finally she strengthened up with a satisfied air and entered the store.

The shadowy interior of Pete Richards's establishment was even more cluttered than his show window. Shelves were stacked with jewel caskets, dueling pistols, clocks and lamps, and the floor was heaped with andirons and mandolins and things hard to find a name for.

Behind the counter stood Pete himself, a man not more than 30 but with hair already turning gray. There was a bleak air about him as he looked at the small customer who flattened her ungloved hands on the counter.

"Mister," she began, "would you please let me look at that string of blue beads in the window?"

Pete parted the draperies and lifted out a necklace. The turquoise stones gleamed brightly against the pallor of his palm as he spread the ornament before her.

"They're just perfect," said the child, entirely to herself. "Will you wrap them up pretty for me, please?"

Pete studied her with a stony air. "Are you buying these for someone?"

"They're for my big sister. She takes care of me.

You see, this will be the first Christmas since Mother died. I've been looking for the most wonderful Christmas present for my sister."

"How much money do you have?" asked Pete warily.

She had been busy untying the knots in a handkerchief and now she poured out a handful of pennies on the counter.

"I emptied my bank," she explained simply.

Pete Richards looked at her thoughtfully. Then he carefully drew back the necklace. The price tag was visible to him but not to her. How could he tell her? The trusting look of her blue eyes smote him like the pain of an old wound.

"Just a minute," he said, and turned toward the back of the store. Over his shoulder he called, "What's your name?" He was very busy about something.

"Jean Grace."

When Pete returned to where Jean Grace waited, a package lay in his hand, wrapped in scarlet paper and tied with a bow of green ribbon. "There you are," he said shortly. "Don't lose it on the way home."

She smiled happily at him over her shoulder as she ran out the door. Through the window he watched her go, while desolation flooded his thoughts. Something about Jean Grace and her string of beads had stirred him to the depths of a grief that would not stay buried. The child's hair was wheat yellow, her eyes were sea blue, and once upon a time, not long before, Pete had been in love with a girl with hair of that same yellow and with eyes just as blue. And the turquoise necklace was to have been hers.

But there had come a rainy night—a truck skidding on a slippery road—and the life was crushed out of his dream.

Since then Pete Richards had lived too much with his grief in solitude. He was politely attentive to customers, but after business hours his world seemed irrevocably empty. He was trying to forget in a self-pitying haze that deepened day by day.

The blue eyes of Jean Grace jolted him into acute remembrance of what he had lost. The pain of it made him recoil from the exuberance of holiday shoppers. During the next ten days trade was brisk; chattering women swarmed in, fingering trinkets, trying to bargain. When the last customer had gone, late on Christmas Eve, he sighed with relief. It was over for another year. But for Pete Richards the night was not quite over.

The door opened and a young woman hurried in. With an inexplicable start, he realized that she looked familiar, yet he could not remember when or where he had seen her before. Her hair was golden yellow and her large eyes were blue. Without speaking she drew from her purse a package loosely unwrapped in its red paper, a bow of green ribbon with it. Presently the string of blue beads lay gleaming again before him.

"Did this come from your shop?" she asked.

Pete raised his eyes to hers and answered softly, "Yes, it did."

"Are the stones real?"

"Yes. Not the finest quality—but real."

"Can you remember who it was you sold them to?"

"She was a small girl. Her name was Jean. She bought them for her older sister's Christmas present."

"How much are they worth?"

"The price," he told her solemnly, "is always a confidential matter between the seller and the customer."

"But Jean has never had more than a few pennies of spending money. How could she pay for them?"

Pete was folding the gay paper back into its creases, rewrapping the little package just as neatly as before.

"She paid the biggest price anyone can ever pay," he said. "She gave all she had."

There was a silence then that filled the little curio shop. In some faraway steeple a bell began to ring. The sound of the distant chiming, the little package lying on the counter, the question in the eyes of the girl and the strange feeling of renewal struggling unreasonably in the heart of the man, all had come to be because of the love of a child.

"But why did you do it?"

He held out the gift in his hand.

"It's already Christmas morning," he said. "And it's my misfortune that I have no one to give anything to. Will you let me see you home and wish you a Merry Christmas at your door?"

And so, to the sound of many bells and in the midst of happy people, Pete Richards and a girl whose name he had yet to learn walked out into the beginning of the great day that brings hope into the world for us all. 🕊

... and a Happy New Year to You, Too!

I'VE ALWAYS wanted a beautiful shawl to wear with my winter dresses. So when I opened the present from my sister Wanda and saw that it was a white-and-silver shawl, I squealed in delight.

"I love it!" I told Wanda that evening. "I wore it all morning."

"You wore it?" she asked, smiling. "It's a skirt for the Christmas tree."

Kay Przybille

• • •

FOR THE holidays one year, rather than send gifts, my friend decided to enclose checks in her greeting cards. Inside each card she wrote "Buy your own presents" and then sent them off.

A few months later, she discovered the checks she'd "mailed" under a pile of books.

Ruth Williams

Night of Hope and Possibility

BY ROXANNE WILLEMS SNOPEK

December 1999

FLICKERING CANDLES glinted on crystal and silverware. Shadows dancing around the table mirrored the excitement in the faces of the children. Each had a carefully folded note tucked secretively next to her plate, awaiting the moment of revelation. For now, though, all was hushed expectation. It was a party, and not just any party. It was New Year's Eve. And for once, they were allowed to stay up.

"WHAT ARE we doing for New Year's Eve, Mom?" nine-year-old Stephanie had asked innocently during breakfast as I was wiping crumbs off the counter. "Nothing," I replied grumpily, thinking of the various invitations my husband, Ray, and I had turned down due to the seasonal babysitter shortage. "We're just staying home."

Stephanie's face fell, and instantly I heard the message I'd just sent. It was, after all, the Christmas season, when social obligations reached fever pitch and many a child kissed a babysitter good night instead of a parent. Parties were for adults, fancy affairs with fancy clothes and expensive food.

I recognized Stephanie's stoic acceptance of her peripheral status, and it stabbed me in the heart. Was this the message I meant to convey? That I stay home with my kids only when there is no better alternative?

I tossed the dishcloth into the sink and turned to my daughter. "Maybe we could have our own party."

Stephanie's eyes lit up, and she ran to tell her two younger sisters.

WE DECIDED on fondue, something the kids had always wanted to try. We whipped through our chores, ran out for the necessary ingredients and began our preparations, an air of festivity percolating among us. As the girls and I sliced bread and grated cheese, we talked about the past year and the important things that had happened.

"You know . . ." I paused for a moment, thinking.

"I'd like to hear more about this when Dad's home, too. Why don't we each write down a few highlights of the past year or the milestones we've reached, and a couple of things we hope for or expect in the new year?"

The girls looked at me dubiously. This sounded like work. "Make sure you keep your list a secret until supper time. Don't tell anyone!" That did it. Each girl ran off with paper and pencil to start her list. Even four-year-old Megan wanted to make one.

THAT EVENING we sat down to a simple meal on a shining table. The usual commotion of mealtime was miraculously suspended, and laughter mingled with the music whenever a chunk of bread was dropped in the fragrant cheese sauce.

"Well, who wants to read her list first?" I looked around the table. Ray and I had made lists, too. "What were some of the year's highlights?"

Stephanie began. "I started piano lessons. We had a great summer and went to the beach. A milestone was learning to cook All By Myself."

Eight-year-old Andrea's list was sprinkled with exclamation marks. "I lost two teeth this year! Christmas was GREAT!!! I met a friend named Hannah at the beach!"

Megan hadn't written her own list, but she was determined to "read" it herself. "I can put my face in the water and blow bubbles," she announced proudly, "and . . . Oh, yeah, I saw a mouse when we were hiking, before anyone else." She sat down triumphantly while her sisters giggled.

Ray cleared his throat. "Celebrating our tenth anniversary was a big highlight for me." He looked over at me and we exchanged a smile. I remembered a time when we wondered if our marriage would make it this far. Only Ray and I knew how much this anniversary signified. It was at the top of my list, too.

We went on to talk about our hopes and expectations for the upcoming year. The girls listed things they wanted to do, skills they hoped to learn or improve, and as they spoke, I saw how much they had changed over the past year. It wouldn't be long until these little girls would be the ones in demand for babysitting on New Year's Eve. How many more chances did we have to celebrate together like this? And how many opportunities had already whisked by, unnoticed?

LATER, WITH the children tucked in bed, Ray and I curled up in front of the fire. The lights twinkling on the Christmas tree added their soft glow to the room, and at that moment the air seemed charged with hope and possibility. This year when someone asks if we have plans for New Year's Eve, I'll tell them we're booked. 🦢

The Holiday I'll Never Forget

December 2011/January 2012

All I'm Asking For

BY RICK BRAGG

I MUST HAVE been about nine years old, too digni-
fied to sit on Santa's lap at the Mason's department
store in Anniston, Alabama, but still young enough
to ask—please, please, please—for a G.I. Joe. "You're
too old to play with dolls," my brother Sam hissed at
me. Sam never was a child. My kin liked to say the
day he was born, he dusted himself off in the delivery
room and walked home.

"G.I. Joe ain't no doll," I hissed back, my face red.

"Is," Sam said.

"Ain't," I said.

That, in Calhoun County, Alabama, in the winter of 1968, is what passed for intellectual discourse.

I was about to pinch him when my tired mother tugged me away to marvel at the fake snow around a deer with pipe cleaners for antlers. Sam marched up to Santa like a little man, presumably to ask for a chain saw and some shotgun shells.

"Do you think I'll get it?" I asked my mother. She was taking in laundry back then, and cleaning houses when she could. Christmas, to her, was a time of great fear, fear that it would be for her three sons a time of great disappointment.

"I don't know, hon," she said, using her other hand to hold tight to my little brother, Mark, who had taken one look at the odd man in the red coat and tried to run for the high country.

"It's all I'm asking for," I said, hopeful.

I didn't know then that just asking was like kicking her in the stomach.

It is hard, when I write of my childhood and Christmas, not to sound a little like Dickens. I am not saying I write that well, just that Christmas, for me as a boy, was always a kind of seesaw of gloom and glee, perhaps the plainest evidence of difference between the classes. A G.I. Joe was a dear thing, a real toy, more than my mother made in a day, some days.

But when I think of those times now, the disappointments seem to lose shape in my mind, and I find instead things that seem, in my second 50 years, much like miracles.

The next day, I moped into my aunt Juanita's kitchen. Aunt Juanita, a tiny woman who could swing a hammer like a man, helped raise me. She fed me peanut butter cookies and fried chicken, though not in that order.

"What's Santy bringing you?" she asked.

"Well," I said, "I wanted a G.I. Joe, but Sam said just girls play with dolls, and I ain't no girl so I reckon I don't want one."

A few days later, I saw a box under her tree with my name on it. She had wrapped it in thin paper, thin enough to see through: G.I. Joe, the one in a sailor's uniform. I wouldn't have cared if he was dressed like an insurance salesman. I spent all the days leading up to Christmas with an odd peace of mind. When I unwrapped it, my mother pretended to be surprised.

Santy, she said, must have conspired with my aunt Juanita.

I love my aunt Juanita for doing that. I love my mother for doing all she could, day after day after day. I know the season means more than this stuff, that it might even be wrong to call such things miracles, even if just tiny ones. The miracle in it, I think, is in those two women's hearts.

The Gift of Possibility

BY ESMERALDA SANTIAGO

THAT CHRISTMAS Eve, the streets of Boston were clogged with tourists and locals bundled in wool and flannel. Shoppers, hawkers and gawkers whirled and swirled around me. "Frosty the Snowman," "Let It Snow!" and "Jingle Bells" played in stores; on the sidewalks, the street musicians did their best. Everyone, it seemed, was accompanied by someone else smiling or laughing. I was alone.

The eldest of a Puerto Rican family of 11 children growing up in New York's crowded tenements, I'd spent much of my life seeking solitude. Now, finally, at 27, a college student in the midst of a drawn-out breakup of a seven-year relationship, I contemplated what I'd so craved, but I wasn't quite sure I liked it. Every part of me wanted to be alone, but not at Christmas.

My family had returned to Puerto Rico, my friends had gone home during the holiday break, and my acquaintances were involved in their own lives. Dusk was falling, and the inevitable return to my empty apartment brought tears to my eyes. Blinking lights from windows and around doors beckoned, and I wished someone would emerge from one of those homes to ask me inside to a warm room with a Christmas tree decorated with tinsel, its velvet skirt sprinkled with shiny fake snow and wrapped presents.

I stopped at the local market, feeling even more depressed as people filled their baskets with goodies. Dates and dried figs, walnuts, pecans and hazelnuts in their shells reminded me of the gifts we received as children in Puerto Rico on Christmas Day, because the big gifts were given on the morning of the Feast of the Epiphany, on January 6. I missed my family: their rambunctious parties; the dancing; the mounds of rice with pigeon peas; the crusty, garlicky skin on the pork roast; the plantain and yucca pasteles wrapped in banana leaves. I wanted to cry for wanting to be alone and for having achieved it.

In front of the church down the street, a manger had been set up, with Mary, Joseph and the barn animals in expectation of midnight and the arrival of baby Jesus. I stood with my neighbors watching the scene, some of them crossing themselves, praying. As I walked home, I realized that the story of Joseph and Mary wandering from door to door seeking shelter was much like my own history. Leaving Puerto Rico was still a wound in my soul as I struggled with who I had become in 15 years in the United States. I'd mourned the losses, but for the first time, I recognized what I'd gained. I was independent, educated, healthy and adventurous. My life was still before me, full of possibility.

Sometimes the best gift is the one you give yourself. That Christmas, I gave myself credit for what I'd accomplished so far and permission to go forward, unafraid. It is the best gift I've ever received, the one that I most treasure.

Eight Candles, Nine Lives
BY MELISSA FAY GREENE

WE PARENTS work so hard to relay the historical and spiritual import of religious holidays. No, we explain, Hanukkah is not primarily about gift giving; it's about a long-ago freedom struggle. The eight-day winter holiday celebrates the successful resistance of the Jews against King Antiochus IV Epiphanes of Syria and the restoration of the Second Temple 21 centuries ago. All our traditions—from lighting the menorah to frying the potato pancakes called latkes to spinning a top in the game of dreidel—contribute to the commemoration of these events.

Unfortunately, the Hanukkah observance that

has stayed with my children as the most significant of their childhoods has nothing to do with religious freedom. One night in the 1990s, we tidied up wrapping paper and toys in the den while the lit menorah stood on the kitchen table. In our absence, as the many-colored candles snapped and dripped, our long-haired black-and-white cat, Ladybug, hopped onto the kitchen table and brushed past them.

"Do you smell something?" asked my husband, Donny.

"Is something burning?" asked Molly, our oldest, age ten.

It was Ladybug! The fur on her left flank had been singed down to the skin. She wasn't hurt, but she wore a peeved expression all evening, and for the rest of the week she hid whenever we began chanting the Hebrew blessings over the candles. Though her fur grew out as thick as ever, Ladybug took a dim view of Hanukkah after that, clearly preferring less flammable holidays, like Labor Day.

The following year, for a fifth-grade assignment about family traditions, Molly wrote about Ladybug's encounter with the Hanukkah candles. The teacher, Lynn Fink, a sporty and funny woman, enjoyed Molly's story and gave it an A.

Three years later, Seth got Ms. Fink for fifth grade. He also worked the scorching of cat fur into a writing assignment, and he, too, got an A.

Ditto our son Lee, three years later: same teacher, same story, same A. We had no idea these retellings were piling up.

The year Lily got Ms. Fink for fifth grade, she also felt inspired to pen an account of the night of a feline afire. By now, we were very fond of Ms. Fink. We invited her to join us for a night of Hanukkah. It was her first time to experience the Jewish holiday. Happily, she ate her latkes with sour cream and applesauce. Gamely, she spun the dreidel. Delightedly, she opened the small gift of homemade cookies the children had prepared for her. As the evening seemed to be winding down, she clapped her hands, rubbed them together as if before a banquet, and exclaimed, "So! When do we torch the cat?"

Sharing the Sweetness
BY TAYARI JONES

ON THE 25th of December, my mother expects her children to be present and accounted for, exchanging gifts and eating turkey. When she pulls on that holiday sweater, everybody better get festive. Of course, I would be the first Jones sibling to go rogue. As the middle, artist child, I was going to strike out and do my own thing, make some new traditions. From a biography of Flannery O'Connor,

I drew inspiration—I would spend the holiday at an artist colony!

No one took the news very well. From the way my mother carried on, you would think that I was divorcing the family. Still, I held my ground and made plans for my winter adventure in New Hampshire. The MacDowell Colony was everything I could have wished for. About 25 to 30 artists were in attendance, and it was as, well, artsy as I had imagined. It felt like my life had become a quirky independent film.

By Christmas Eve, I had been at the colony more than a week. The novelty of snowy New England was wearing off, but I would never admit it. Everyone around me was having too much fun. Sledding and bourbon! Deep conversations by the fireplace! And that guy with the piercings. So cute! What was wrong with me? This was the holiday I'd always dreamed of. No plastic reindeer grazing on the front lawn. No football games on TV. Not a Christmas sweater anywhere in sight. People here didn't even say "Christmas," they said "holiday." Utter sophistication. Then why was I so sad?

Finally, I called home on the pay phone in the common room. My dad answered, but I could barely hear him for all the good-time noise in the background. He turned down the volume on the Stevie Wonder holiday album and told me that my mother was out shopping with my brothers. Now it was my turn to sulk. They were having a fine Christmas without me.

Despite a massive blizzard, a large package showed up near my door at the artist colony on Christmas morning. *Tayari Jones* was written in my mother's beautiful handwriting. I pounced on that parcel like I was five years old. Inside was a gorgeous red-velvet cake, my favorite, swaddled in about 50 yards of bubble wrap. *Merry Christmas,* read the simple card inside. *We love you very much.*

As I sliced the cake, everyone gathered around— the young and the old, the cynical and the earnest. Mother had sent a genuine homemade gift, not trendy or ironic. It was a minor Christmas miracle that one cake managed to feed so many. We ate it from paper towels with our bare hands, satisfying a hunger we didn't know we had.

Some Assembly Required
BY FLOYD SKLOOT

MY FIVE-YEAR-OLD daughter knew exactly what she wanted for Christmas of 1977, and told me so. Yes, she still would like the pink-and-green plastic umbrella with a clear top she'd been talking about. Great to observe patterns of rain spatters. Books, long flannel nightgown, fuzzy slippers—fine. But really, there was only one thing that mattered: a Barbie Townhouse, with all the accessories.

This was a surprise. Rebecca was not a Barbie girl, preferred stuffed animals to dolls and wasn't drawn to play in a structured environment. Always a make-up-the-rules, design-your-own-world, do-it-my-way kid. Maybe, I thought, the point wasn't Barbie but house, a domicile she could claim for herself, since we'd already moved five times during her brief life.

Next day, I stopped at the mall. The huge Barbie Townhouse box was festooned with exclamations: *"3 Floors of High-Styled Fun! Elevator Can Stop on All Floors!" Some Assembly Required.*

Uh-oh. My track record for assembling things was miserable. Brooklyn-born, I was raised in apartment buildings in a family that didn't build things. A few years earlier, I'd spent one week assembling a six-foot-tall jungle gym from a kit containing so many parts, I spent the first four hours sorting and weeping and the last two hours trying to figure out why there were so many leftover pieces. The day after I finished building it, as if to remind me of my limitations, a tornado touched down close enough to scatter the jungle gym across an acre of field.

I assembled the Barbie Townhouse on Christmas Eve. Making it level, keeping the columns from looking like they'd melted and been refrozen, and getting that elevator to work were almost more than I could manage. And building it in curse-free silence so my daughter would continue sleeping—if, in fact, she was sleeping—added a layer of challenge. By dawn I was done.

Shortly thereafter, my daughter walked into the living room, stuffed bear tucked under her arm, feigning shock and looking as tired as I did. Her surprise may have been sham, but her delight was utterly genuine and moves me to this day, 34 years later. Rebecca had spurred me to do something I didn't think I could do. It was for her, and—like so much of the privilege of being her father—it brought me further outside myself and let me overcome doubts about my capacities.

Now that I think about it, there probably was real surprise in her first glimpse of her Barbie Townhouse. Not, perhaps, at the gift itself but that it had been built and remained standing in the morning light. Or maybe it was simpler than that: Maybe she was surprised because she'd planned on building the thing herself.

A Legacy of Love
BY LEE SMITH

DECEMBER 23, 1969. When it gets really cold down South, it seems colder than anyplace else. It had been freezing out in the piney woods the day we cut down our Christmas tree—

which had been decorated for weeks now in the living room of our little frame house in Tuscaloosa, Alabama. I remember the pattern of glittery frost on our uninsulated windows, the chilly wind that slipped under the doors, the sound of our steps as we crunched across the frozen grass of our front yard early that morning. We'd been up for most of the night, timing the pains. I looked back as my young husband gunned the car out of the driveway, headed for the hospital. In the bright morning sun, ice glittered on every branch of every silver tree.

Two people live in that house now, I remember thinking. Soon there will be three.

Six pounds, seven ounces, he came in hollering at the top of his lungs; he had ten fingers and ten toes and a funny flat nose and a pointed head. Just an ordinary, healthy baby boy: a miracle. We named him Josh.

Soon they took him away so that I could rest, but I couldn't sleep a wink—I was way too excited. When they wheeled him back, he was wearing a bright red Santa hat. A red-and-white felt Christmas stocking hung from his bassinet.

I have that little hat and stocking still.

We don't have Josh, though. He died in his sleep eight years ago, October 26, 2003. The exact cause of his death was an "acute myocardiopathy," the collapse of an enlarged heart brought about in part, I believe, by all the weight he had gained while taking anti-psychotic drugs. He was 34; he had been sick for half his life doing daily heroic battle with the devastating brain disorder—schizophrenia—that first struck while he was in a program for gifted teen musicians at Berklee College of Music in Boston, the summer between his junior and senior years in high school.

Yet we don't mourn Josh at Christmastime but celebrate his remarkable life.

Thanks to early diagnosis and medical treatment, which included hospitalization, a residential outpatient program, and vocational training, Josh was eventually able to live on his own. He learned to manage his medication and get to his doctor appointments on time. For the last seven years of his life, he worked at a Japanese restaurant, where he made sushi for lunch and often played piano at night, a mix of jazz, blues and his own compositions.

What a privilege it was to live on this earth with him, to be his mother. Of course, to have children—or simply to experience great love for any person at all—is to throw yourself wide open to the possibility of pain at any moment. But I would never choose otherwise.

Now we have four grandchildren, two of them his namesakes. And this holiday, as always, we will hang Josh's bright little Santa hat and worn red felt stocking on our Christmas tree.

Merry, Silly Christmas
BY JENNY ALLEN

MY BEST Christmas was the year we had Ken and Barbie at the top of our tree. We had an angel first, for Christmas Day, but then we had Ken and Barbie. Let me explain. When my daughter was four, I hired a ballet dancer to babysit for a few afternoons a week. Randy was tall and confident, with that dancer's chest-first carriage, and, though he was only 27, a sure, cheerful bossiness. For four years, he and Halley roamed the city on adventures: to climb the Alice in Wonderland statue in Central Park, to smile at the waddling, pint-sized penguins at the zoo. They had their own world, their own passions: a devotion to ice cream, to Elmo, to Pee-wee Herman.

He orchestrated Halley's birthday parties to a fare-thee-well: One year he declared a Peter Pan theme, made Halley a Tinker Bell outfit with little jingle bells at the hem, and talked my father into making a scary appearance in a big-brimmed pirate hat and a fake hook for a hand. Randy took charge of my grown-up parties, too, dictating what I wore, foraging in thrift shops to find the right rhinestone necklace to go with the dress he'd made me buy.

When Halley was eight, Randy left New York to take over a sleepy ballet company in a small city in Colorado.

He taught, he choreographed, he coaxed secretaries and computer salesmen into pliéing across the stage.

Halley missed him terribly—we all did—but he called her and sent her party dresses, and he came to see us at Christmas when he could. The year Halley was ten, we had a new baby. That same year, Randy was diagnosed with AIDS. He told me over the phone, without an ounce of self-pity, that he had so few T cells left that he'd named them Huey, Dewey and Louie.

It seemed insane for him to travel, insane for him to risk one of us sneezing on him and giving him pneumonia, but he had decided, and that was it. He was as cheerful and bossy as ever. Terribly thin, his cheeks hollow but eyes bright, he took Halley all over the city once again, with baby Julie strapped to his chest in a cloth carrier.

"We've got to do something about this tree," he said one day. The tree, with its red ribbon bows, looked fine to me; I was even a little vain about the way every branch shone with ornaments.

A few days later, on New Year's Eve morning, he summoned our little family. He was wearing the old pirate's hat, fished out of a costume box and, for hair, curly colored streamers that stuck out of the hat and tumbled down to his shoulders.

As we watched—me irritable at first, wondering how much you were supposed to yield to a dying houseguest, even if you loved him like a brother—he stripped the tree. Then he brought out more curly streamers, heaps of them, and tooters and little party-favor plastic champagne bottles. "Now we'll turn it into a New Year's tree," he declared.

A New Year's tree! Of course! We threw the streamers all over the tree, we covered it with the tooters and the tiny champagne bottles. "And now, for the pièce de résistance," Randy said. Stretching his tall self way up to the top of the tree, he removed its gold papier-mâché angel. Solemnly, carefully, he placed on top Halley's tuxedoed Ken and her best Barbie, the one in a sparkly ball gown.

"Ta da!" he said, and beamed. It was a wonderful tree, happy and goofy and perfect.

Randy lived for another year and a half. None of us will ever get over his death, not really. But every Christmastime, I raise a glass to Randy—to his tree, to his bossiness, to the Christmas he taught us that courage is a man in a pirate hat with silly streamers for hair. 🦢

Dressed to Kill

ONE MID-OCTOBER evening, I answered a knock on the door. There in front of me was a boy wearing a Dracula mask. "Trick or treat!" he yelled.

"Nice costume," I said. "But Halloween's not for another two weeks."

"I know," he said. "But I'm away then."   *Jim Robertson*

Christmas Out of Season

August 1998

FROM *All I Really Need to Know I Learned in Kindergarten*

ONE YEAR I didn't receive many Christmas cards. This troublemaking realization actually came to me one fetid February afternoon out of the back room in my head that is the source of useless information. Guess I needed some reason to really feel crummy, so there it was. But I didn't say anything about it. I can take it. I am tough. I won't complain when my cheap friends don't even care enough to send me a stupid Christmas card. I can do without love. Right.

The following August, I was nesting in the attic,

trying to establish some order in the mess, and found stacked in with the holiday decorations a whole box of unopened greeting cards from the previous Christmas. I had tossed them into the box to open at leisure, and then I ran out of leisure in the shambles of the usual Christmas panic, so they got caught up in the bale-it-up-and-stuff-it-in-the-attic-and-we'll-straighten-it-out-next-year syndrome.

I hauled the box down, and on a hot mid-August day, mind you, in my bathing suit, sitting in a lawn chair on my deck, with sunglasses, cocoa butter, a quart of iced tea and a puzzled frame of mind, I began to open my Christmas cards. Just to help, I had put a tape of Christmas carols on the portable stereo and cranked up the volume.

Here it all was. Angels, snow, Wise Men, candles and pine boughs, horses and sleighs, the Holy Family, elves and Santa. Messages about love and joy and peace and good will. If that wasn't enough, there were all those handwritten messages of affections from my cheap friends who had, in fact, come through for the holidays.

I cried. Seldom have I felt so bad and so good at the same time. So wonderfully rotten, elegantly sad, and melancholy and nostalgic and all.

As fate always seems to have it, I was discovered in this condition by a neighbor, who had been attracted to the scene by the sound of Christmas caroling. She laughed. I showed her the cards. She cried. And we had this outrageous Christmas ordeal right there on my deck in the middle of August, singing along with the Mormon Tabernacle Choir to the mighty strains of "O Holy Night": "Faaallll on your kneeees, O heeeeear the angel vooiiicees."

What can I say? I guess wonder and awe and joy are always there in the attic of one's mind somewhere, and it doesn't take a lot to set it off. And much about Christmas is outrageous, whether it comes to you in December or in the heat of an August day. 🕊

Feast or Family

I WAS a vegetarian until I married a proud meat eater. On Christmas, as our children gathered around the table, my husband announced, "Your mother didn't know what a turkey was until she met me."   *Lorraine Larkin*

• • •

DURING THE holidays, my daughter-in-law Heather called to ask me for a fruitcake recipe. As I looked it up, she mentioned that she had told some friends about the cakes she was making, and one of them asked her how she learned to make them. "Easy," Heather told her. "I called my mother-in-law. She's the queen of fruitcakes!"
Pam Northcott

Healin
Healing
Healing
Healing

A Love Like No Other

BY SKIP HOLLANDSWORTH

May 1995

CONDENSED FROM *Texas Monthly*

ROM THE day she was born, doctors had expected Kimberley Marshall to die. She had cystic fibrosis, a baffling genetic disorder. Desperate to keep her baby alive, Kim's mother, Dawn, took the infant home and for three hours a day she and Kim's grandmother gently thumped on her chest and back to dislodge the sticky mucus that clogs the lungs of CF patients. Trying to get rid of it, one doctor says, is like sweeping spilled molasses off the floor with a broom.

To everyone's astonishment, Kim eventually grew strong enough to go to elementary school. She even took ballet lessons and joined a girls' soccer team.

"There goes the princess," Dawn would shout from the sidelines, momentarily allowing herself to feel as normal as the other mothers. She imagined Kim to be normal, too, the kind of girl who might go to a high-school dance and lift her head dreamily at the end of the night, as a boy gave her her first kiss.

But Robert Kramer, the first doctor in Dallas to specialize in CF, warned Dawn and her husband, Bill, that it was only a temporary reprieve. Like a serial killer, CF is unstoppable. Although an array of pulmonary treatments and medicines now allows patients to live more productive, pain-free lives, average life expectancy is about 29 years.

AS DR. Kramer predicted, the days soon came when Kim's body seemed to deflate like a rubber toy with a hole in it, and Dawn would return her to the Presbyterian Hospital of Dallas. The routine became all too familiar: a few months of remission followed by a trip to the hospital's CF unit.

Kim always brought along her stuffed animals, her favorite pink blanket and her diary. As children around her died, she'd write down her impressions ("Wendy died at 8:10 this morning! She suffered all night. It's better this way. Poor little thing"). It was, Dawn thought, Kim's way of preparing herself for what she knew would someday happen to her.

For a while Kim did what she could to be like the "normals" (her nickname for kids without CF). In high school she earned A's and B's and wore long dresses to hide her spindly legs. When classmates asked about her coughing spells, she would say she suffered from asthma. She'd pick up other CF girls in her car and drive along, honking her horn, waving at boys and flashing a jubilant smile.

Still, she could not ignore the reality of her life. Her digestive system was so clogged with mucus that she suffered painful attacks of diarrhea. She developed a neurological disorder that affected her balance and distorted her perception.

Finally, during her senior year, she grew so weak that she had to finish her course work at home. In one of her lowest moments she asked that her picture not be included in her high-school yearbook. "I look like a starvation victim," she said. Growing increasingly frustrated, Kim argued often with her younger brother and sister. Over and over she watched a videotape of *The Blue Lagoon,* the story of an adolescent boy and girl who are stranded on an island and fall in love.

DAVID CRENSHAW first laid eyes on Kim in the spring of 1986 when both were being treated at Presbyterian. She was 16, thin, pale and beautiful, her red hair falling down the back of her pink nightgown. David was

18. He wore a baggy T-shirt, faded gray pajama pants and large glasses held together by a piece of tape.

"No way she's going to look twice at you," teased Doug Kellum, one of the CF unit's respiratory therapists, who had noticed David staring at her. And, indeed, it was difficult to imagine any attraction between them. Kim loved expensive perfume, makeup and clothes. She would sit for hours in her hospital bed, reading romance novels.

David, on the other hand, was famous for trying to impress girls with crude jokes. Loud and robust, he was something of a legend at Presbyterian. No one had ever heard of a CF patient doing the things David did. For instance, when he wasn't in the hospital, he raced midget cars at a local dirt track. "Our goal was to raise him as if he weren't sick," says David's father. "Maybe I thought if he stayed tough enough, he could beat it."

In truth, David never did act particularly sick. A prankster, he conducted wheelchair races and tomato-throwing competitions in the hospital's third-floor hallway. One night he took some CF patients to a go-cart track in 32-degree weather. "He had this sense of immortality about him," Dr. Kramer remembers.

For two years David would often walk past Kim's door, working up the courage to pop in and say hello. Kim would look at him, smile briefly, then go back to reading her book.

David was undaunted. "When she was in the hospital and he was home," Kellum says, "he'd call me to find out how she was—even though she wouldn't give him the time of day."

Surprisingly, it is often in the CF unit that young patients experience their first encounter with romance. "You assume that because CF kids look so weak, they don't have much of a sex drive," says Dr. Kramer. "Yet they probably think about it more than regular people. It's their way of affirming to themselves that they are alive and kicking."

In late 1988 Kim began an on-again, off-again relationship with another CF patient, a young man named Steve. "I knew it wasn't going to work out," David said. "They were afraid of commitment." And the relationship did finally falter.

In the fall of 1989, when he and Kim were both at home once again, David called and asked her to dinner. Although she said no, David declared, "I'll be there at 8 p.m., no buts about it."

Horrified, Kim brought along her sister, Petri, and made her sit with David in the front seat of his car while she sat in the back, refusing to speak. Kim also remained silent through dinner, and gave David a tortured look when he suggested they go dancing at a nightclub. When he took her home, Kim leapt out of the car and ran to her room.

Still, David kept showing up at Kim's house. They

went bowling. He took her to watch him race. And, despite everything, love bloomed. On November 17, 1989, Kim wrote in her diary: "Tonight, David and I kissed for the first time. God, please let this relationship work out."

Six months after their first date, Kim and David announced their engagement—to the shock of their families, friends and doctors. "Both of you are sick," David's father said, pleading with him to reconsider. "You can't possibly take care of yourselves." "Do you realize that one of you is going to die in the other's arms?" Dawn asked her daughter tearfully.

Kim and David insisted that they had a right to be together. "I think Kim realized this was going to be the last chance she had to experience love," Dawn said, finally agreeing to the union.

On October 27, 1990, Kim Marshall, 21, wobbled down the aisle and declared her love for 23-year-old David Crenshaw. The church was filled with the sound of coughing, as Dallas's CF community came to support them.

THE COUPLE lived on their modest monthly disability checks in a one-bedroom apartment. It resembled a hospital room, crammed with oxygen tanks, medicines and a refrigerator stocked with I.V. bottles.

Domestic tasks were difficult: They needed a day to clean the apartment and do the laundry. By nighttime both were exhausted. Yet they were happier than they ever could have imagined. He nicknamed her Tigger (from the children's book *Winnie the Pooh*) because of her red hair; she called him Bear because he was cuddly. He was always sending her cards, the mushier the better. She wrote him long love letters. ("We are going to conquer the unconquerable.")

To earn extra income, David worked rebuilding race cars. He also enrolled at a junior college to get an accounting degree. One of his CF friends, Richard Johnson, warned him it was impossible to keep up such a pace. David just said, "I've got to do this for Kim. There isn't anything in my life but her."

By 1992 Kim's veins had begun to collapse. Because her body was unable to absorb food through her clogged digestive system, she was rapidly losing weight. She became ashamed to show herself in public. "Tigger," David wrote her, "you are the most beautiful woman I know inside and out. I love you with all my heart and soul! Bear."

David never left Kim's side during her frequent trips to the hospital. He would sleep on a cot in her room. To entertain her, he wheeled her to the maternity ward so she could look at the babies. If she wanted candy in the middle of the night, he'd go out and buy her some. Amazingly, Kim's health improved, and she returned home.

Then, in early 1993, David's condition worsened.

His cough grew louder and deeper. His face got puffy from fluid retention. Eventually he, too, breathed with the assistance of a portable oxygen machine.

David assured Kim there was nothing to worry about; he just had to build up his strength. He didn't tell her what Dr. Kramer had said after a recent checkup: David's lungs were becoming stiff with scar tissue and his bronchial tubes were closing up. He was slowly choking to death.

It was a race against time, and David would not waste a single moment. In July, to celebrate his 26th birthday and Kim's 24th, he insisted they take a week-long Florida vacation. "Only once did they feel good enough to leave the condo and go to the beach," says Kim's sister, Mandy, who traveled with them. "Both carried their portable oxygen tanks. They sat on the beach holding hands."

Three months later, David and Kim went for a checkup. While Kim waited in another room, Dr. Kramer studied David's oxygen levels. "You've got to go into the hospital," he said. "And this time, you may be there for a long time." David managed only one response: "Make sure Kim is okay."

Kramer walked across the hall to tell her. Kim dropped her head and tried not to cry. "Don't let him suffer, Dr. Bob," she said. During his 30 years as a CF specialist, Kramer had watched more than 400 young patients die. For his own sanity, he distanced himself emotionally from cases like David's. But now he gathered Kim in his arms and wept.

David was admitted to the hospital on October 21. Kim sat by his side. She tried to write a letter to Medicare officials, begging them to consider him for a lung transplant, a last resort for a few CF patients, but she never got to finish it. Five days later, David's lips and fingernails turned blue.

"David, not yet," she said. Unable to speak, he mouthed "I love you" and blew her a kiss. Kim and David exchanged one long look of grief and love. Moments later he died.

Within 24 hours of his funeral, Kim went into a state of shock. A week later Dawn took her to the hospital. After seeing her, Dr. Kramer offered a decidedly unmedical diagnosis to her parents. "Her body is giving up," he told them. "It's as if she were dying of a broken heart."

Kim was semicomatose for two days. Then, early on the morning of November 11, she regained consciousness, opened her eyes and began speaking in a peaceful, cooing voice that no one could understand. A nurse said it sounded as if she were talking to David. Then she shut her eyes and died.

Kim was buried in her wedding dress alongside her husband. Their tombstone reads: "David S. (Bear) Crenshaw and Kimberley (Tigger) Crenshaw . . . Together forever. Married three years."

All their friends and family agreed theirs had been a love story like no other. "To me," said Dr. Kramer, "it was Romeo and Juliet all over again."

Weeks later, Dawn was sorting through the couple's possessions. She came across the last card David had sent Kim before he died. "We are close even when we are apart," it read. "Just look up. We are both under the same starry sky." 🕊

Wanted: The Healing Power of a Pet

THIS CLASSIFIED ad from the *Sturgis* (Michigan) *Journal* showcases a cat that thinks it's a lion. "Free to good home: 2 adult female cats, 1 long-haired gray, 1 deluded calico."
Linda Meggison

• • •

MY WIFE found this flyer taped to a neighborhood telephone pole: "Found, male yellow Lab, very friendly. Loves to play with kids and eat Bubbles. Bubbles is our cat. Please come get your dog."
Robert Chapman

• • •

WHO COULD resist this dog after the sales pitch in the *Athens* (Ohio) *News*? "Worst dog ever. Free to a good home. Not fixed. Doesn't come when called. Runs away. Kills chickens and has foul smell."
Laura Calentine

Two Words to Avoid, Two to Remember

BY ARTHUR GORDON

January 1968

NOTHING IN life is more exciting and rewarding than the sudden flash of insight that leaves
you a changed person—not only changed, but
changed for the better. Such moments are rare, certainly, but they come to all of us. Sometimes from a
book, a sermon, a line of poetry. Sometimes from a
friend. . . .

That wintry afternoon in Manhattan, waiting in
the little French restaurant, I was feeling frustrated
and depressed. Because of several miscalculations on
my part, a project of considerable importance in my

life had fallen through. Even the prospect of seeing a dear friend (the Old Man, as I privately and affectionately thought of him) failed to cheer me as it usually did. I sat there frowning at the checkered tablecloth, chewing the bitter cud of hindsight.

He came across the street, finally, muffled in his ancient overcoat, shapeless felt hat pulled down over his bald head, looking more like an energetic gnome than an eminent psychiatrist. His office was nearby; I knew he had just left his last patient of the day. He was close to 80, but he still carried a full caseload, still acted as director of a large foundation, still loved to escape to the golf course whenever he could.

By the time he came over and sat beside me, the waiter had brought his invariable bottle of ale. I had not seen him for several months, but he seemed as indestructible as ever. "Well, young man," he said without preliminary, "what's troubling you?"

I had long since ceased to be surprised at his perceptiveness. So I proceeded to tell him, at some length, just what was bothering me. With a kind of melancholy pride, I tried to be very honest, I blamed no one else for my disappointment, only myself. I analyzed the whole thing, all the bad judgements, the false moves. I went on for perhaps 15 minutes, while the Old Man sipped his ale in silence.

When I finished, he put down his glass. "Come on," he said. "Let's go back to my office."

"Your office? Did you forget something?"

"No," he said mildly. "I want your reaction to something. That's all."

A chill rain was beginning to fall outside, but his office was warm and comfortable and familiar: book-lined walls, long leather couch, signed photograph of Sigmund Freud, tape recorder by the window. His secretary had gone home. We were alone.

The Old Man took a tape from a flat cardboard box and fitted it onto the machine. "On this tape," he said, "are three short recordings made by three persons who came to me for help. They are not identified, of course. I want you to listen to the recordings and see if you can pick out the two-word phrase that is the common denominator in all three cases." He smiled. "Don't look so puzzled. I have my reasons."

What the owners of the voices on the tape had in common, it seemed to me, was unhappiness. The man who spoke first evidently had suffered some kind of business loss or failure; he berated himself for not having worked harder, for not having looked ahead. The woman who spoke next had never married because of a sense of obligation to her widowed mother; she recalled bitterly all the marital chances she had let go by. The third voice belonged to a mother whose teenage son was in trouble with the police; she blamed herself endlessly.

The Old Man switched off the machine and leaned

back in his chair. "Six times in those recordings a phrase is used that's full of a subtle poison. Did you spot it? No? Well, perhaps that's because you used it three times yourself down in the restaurant a little while ago." He picked up the box that had held the tape and tossed it over to me. "There they are, right on the label. The two saddest words in any language."

I looked down. Printed neatly in red ink were the words: *If only*.

"You'd be amazed," said the Old Man, "if you knew how many thousands of times I've sat in this chair and listened to the woeful sentences beginning with those two words. 'If only,' they say to me, 'I had done it differently—or not done it at all. If only I hadn't lost my temper, said that cruel thing, made that dishonest move, told that foolish lie. If only I had been wiser, or more unselfish, or more self-controlled.' They go on and on until I stop them. Sometimes I make them listen to the recordings you just heard. 'If only,' I say to them, 'you'd stop saying *if only*, we might begin to get somewhere!'"

The Old Man stretched out his legs. "The trouble with 'if only,'" he said, "is that it doesn't change anything. It keeps the person facing the wrong way—backward instead of forward. It wastes time. In the end, if you let it become a habit, it can become a real roadblock, an excuse for not trying anymore.

"Now take your own case: your plans didn't work out. Why? Because you made certain mistakes. Well, that's all right: everyone makes mistakes. Mistakes are what we learn from. But when you were telling me about them, lamenting this, regretting that, you weren't really learning from them."

"How do you know?" I said, a bit defensively.

"Because," said the Old Man, "you never got out of the past tense. Not once did you mention the future. And in a way—be honest, now!—you were enjoying it. There's a perverse streak in all of us that makes us like to hash over old mistakes. After all, when you relate the story of some disaster or disappointment that has happened to you, you're still the chief character, still in the center of the stage."

I shook my head ruefully. "Well, what's the remedy?"

"Shift the focus," said the Old Man promptly. "Change the key words and substitute a phrase that supplies life instead of creating drag."

"Do you have such a phrase to recommend?"

"Certainly. Strike out the words 'if only'; substitute the phrase 'next time.'"

"*Next time?*"

"That's right. I've seen it work minor miracles right here in this room. As long as a patient keeps saying 'if only' to me, he's in trouble. But when he looks me in the eye and says 'next time,' I know he's on his way to overcoming his problem. It means he has decided to apply the lessons he has learned from his experience, however grim or painful it may have been. It means he's going to push aside the roadblock of regret, move forward, take action, resume living. Try it yourself. You'll see."

My old friend stopped speaking. Outside, I could hear the rain whispering against the windowpane. I tried sliding one phrase out of my mind and replacing it with the other. It was fanciful, of course, but I could hear the new words lock into place with an audible click.

"One last thing," the Old Man said. "Apply this little trick to things that can still be remedied." From the bookcase behind him he pulled out something that looked like a diary. "Here's a journal kept a generation ago by a woman who was a schoolteacher in my hometown. Her husband was a kind of amiable ne'er-do-well, charming but totally inadequate as a provider. This woman had to raise the children, pay the bills, keep the family together. Her diary is full of angry references to Jonathan's inadequacies.

"Then Jonathan died, and all the entries ceased except for one—years later. Here it is: 'Today I was made superintendent of schools, and I suppose I should be very proud. But if I knew that Jonathan was out there somewhere beyond the stars, and if I knew how to manage it, I would go to him tonight.' "

The Old Man closed the book gently. "You see? What she's saying is 'if only; if only,' I had accepted him, faults and all; if only I had loved him while I could." He put the book back on the shelf. "That's when those sad words are the saddest of all: when it's too late to retrieve anything."

He stood up a bit stiffly. "Well, class dismissed. It has been good to see you young man. Always is. Now, if you will help me find a taxi, I probably should be getting on home."

We came out of the building into the rainy night. I spotted a cruising cab and ran toward it, but another pedestrian was quicker.

"My, my," said the Old Man slyly. "If only we had come down ten seconds sooner, we'd have caught the cab, wouldn't we?"

I laughed and picked up the cue. "Next time I'll run faster."

"That's it," cried the Old Man, pulling his absurd hat down around his ears. "That's it exactly!"

Another taxi slowed. I opened the door for him. He smiled and waved as it moved away. I never saw him again. A month later, he died of a sudden heart attack, in full stride, so to speak.

Much time has passed since that rainy afternoon

in Manhattan. But to this day, whenever I find my-self thinking "if only," I change it to "next time." Then I wait for the almost-perceptible mental click. And when I hear it, I think of the Old Man.

A small fragment of immortality, to be sure. But it's the kind he would have wanted. 🦢

Problem Solved

ANTHONY MILLER was acting oddly, even for a rob-ber, when he entered a bank in Ephrata, Pennsylvania. He drew his BB gun, demanded money, and then asked the teller to call the police. Miller later explained that he wanted to be arrested so he could get away from his wife. It worked. He was sentenced to three to six years in prison.   *Source: Associated Press*

• • •

WHILE I was visiting my grandfather in the hospital, a nurse came in to check his blood sugar. Before she started, the nurse examined his red fingertips, which had been poked numerous times already, and said, "Hmm . . . which finger should we use this time that won't hurt too much?"

"Yours," my grandfather replied.   *Tara Vyn*

The Day My Silent Brother Spoke

BY JIM WATSON

January 1992

T WAS my mother's wedding day—a hot July morning in a small stone church in the foothills of Virginia's Blue Ridge Mountains. She was 60 and never more radiant as she opened this new chapter in her life. Outside the church, Mother called us together for a few serious words.

"Go see Grandma now," she said. "Don't be upset if she doesn't know you." Strokes and heart disease had left my 89-year-old grandmother lying crumpled and uncomprehending in a nursing-home bed.

As I drove through town, I looked around at my passengers. Here we were, the grandchildren: a banker, an entrepreneur, a musician, a lawyer, a journalist. And next to the window in the backseat, sitting quietly, was Page. How could this affect him? Probably not at all. He would never understand.

PAGE, MY younger brother by four years, has been brain-damaged from birth. He does not speak, cannot hear and sees poorly through his remaining eye. He stopped growing when he was five feet tall and struggles against obesity. A wall of autism shuts him away from the outside world. He spends most of his time lost in his own musings, nodding, laughing, clucking and crying at a pageant only he can see.

Growing up, his brothers played football, drove cars, made friends and dated pretty girls. Page stayed home, entertaining himself on a rope swing, staring at television or playing with a flashlight—his life-long fascination. One by one, the rest of us went off to school, got jobs, married and moved away. Page traveled to dreary institutions and rehabilitation centers, where he learned the basics of reading and using tools. Now 34, he has a room in a private home and a job with a small workshop for people like him. He is on his own, and at last he is happy. But it wasn't always this way.

During his teens, Page struggled with the

emotional overload of adolescence. Seized by fits of anger, he would burst into uncontrollable tears, rake his fingernails down his face until his cheeks bled or, frustrated by newly forming cataracts, jab at his eyes with pencils. He passed through several distinct phases, each marked by a peculiar ritual.

First there was ground-kissing. Every so often, for no apparent reason, he would stop in midstep, drop to his knees and give the floor or sidewalk a long, passionate kiss. Wiping the dirt from his lips, he would calmly stand up and, with an air of accomplishment, continue on his way.

Ground-kissing gave way to spinning in place. From a sitting position, Page would suddenly stand up, twirl around as if he were unwinding himself from an invisible string and then, satisfied, take his seat. He whirled three times—never more, never less. One Sunday in church, Page decided to "unravel" during the sermon. First, a rustle of papers and clothes. Then he stood, knocking a hymnal loudly to the floor. All eyes turned to investigate the disturbance. Children gawked, bewildered. I stared at the church bulletin, my face burning.

FOR YEARS, my reaction to Page's behavior was embarrassment, anger, resentment. Why him? Why me? I was sure he saved his most humiliating stunts for when we were in public. People stared. Page was strange. Did they think there was something strange about our whole family—about me?

As I got older, however, I began to understand that he had no control over his actions, that I could not judge him as I judge others. He wasn't trying to be difficult or strange. He was simply lost, never to be found.

As he drifted further away, I gave up trying to recover the brother I had been denied. Shame and anger turned into acceptance. In time, if I caught anyone staring at the frowning, clucking little fat man with hearing aids in both ears and pockets bulging with flashlights and magnifying glasses, I stared back defiantly.

JUST BEFORE we left for the nursing home, Mom had penciled the words "VISIT GRANDMA" for Page in large letters on a napkin. Yet no one expected him to grasp our purpose, to understand that this might be our last visit.

As I drove, other memories floated through my mind: memories of 80-year-old Grandma, arms like sticks, pushing her old power mower up the slope of her backyard, dismissing able-bodied volunteers with a shrug. Grandma's thin, shaking fingers carefully unwrapping Christmas presents to avoid tearing the paper, which she folded neatly by her side. And, of course, talking. Always talking.

The sound of Grandma's voice accompanies every memory of her. She spoke not in sentences or even paragraphs, but in entire chapters, convoluted and strung together by breathless "ands," "buts" and "anyways." We seldom asked questions for fear of opening the faucet. Instead, we listened, playing polite audience, nodding at appropriate moments even as we calculated how to steer her back to the subject (if we could remember it) or blurt out a quick thought of our own. "Oh, I *know* I talk too much," she would sometimes sigh. "Your mother tells me I do."

While Grandma could not listen and Page could not talk, they understood each other perfectly. In his silent fortress, Page was unaware of the impenetrable wall of words Grandma built around herself. She kissed him and smiled at him and, more important, accepted him just as he was. She never showed disappointment that he was not "normal," but rather regarded him with fascination, patience and warmth.

One day Page broke a flashlight and brought it to her, hoping she could fix it. I remember her perplexed, earnest face as she fumbled with the cheap plastic gadget. She poked and wiggled the thing and finally, looking sorrowful, shook her head and handed it back to Page. He walked away, to return a few minutes later and try again. She fumbled some more, then gave it back; it was still broken. The next morning Grandma drove to the store and bought him a new one.

WE ARRIVED at the nursing home and stepped into her room. The strokes had left Grandma trembling and unresponsive. The hollow, gaping mask that stared up from her pillow was the face of a wizened stranger. Her mouth hung open. Her wide misty eyes blinked and stared but appeared not to see.

I patted her small, frail hand, and my mind filled with images from a not-so-distant past. This very hand used to produce steaming loaves of the best bread on God's earth. This patient, loving hand didn't stop waving from Grandma's front porch until our car, packed with grandchildren, disappeared around the corner. Now lying limply by her side, her delicate, cool hand felt so soft I was afraid I might accidentally hurt her.

We stood around the bed, smiling uncomfortably, mumbling everything would be all right. My older cousin was the most at ease. "They treatin' you all right in this place, ol' girl?" he asked. I watched her face closely for a sign of recognition. Nothing. Silence didn't suit Grandma.

Stripped of her verbal armor, Grandma seemed exposed, vulnerable and—as I realized with sadness—suddenly approachable. For the first time, I was free to talk all I wanted. But I could think of nothing to say.

"We love you, Grandma," I said finally, wondering if I was reaching her. My words hung in the air, sounding distant and insincere.

Page was standing quietly next to the window, his face brilliant red, tears streaming from his eyes. Just then, he pushed through the group and made his way to the bed. He leaned over Grandma's withered figure and took her cheeks gently in his hands. Head bowed, he stood there for an eternity, cradling her face and soaking her gown with his tears. Those of us with healthy ears were deaf to the volumes being spoken in that wonderful, wordless exchange.

I felt a rush of warmth deep inside me. It surged upward like an inexorable flood, filling my eyes until the room melted in a wash of colors and liquid shapes. As the picture blurred, my perception snapped into brilliant focus. How wrong I had been about Page. Far better than the rest of us, he knew the true meaning of our visit. He knew it perfectly because he grasped it not with his head but with his heart. Like a child unrestrained by propriety or ego, he had the freedom, courage and honesty to reach out in pain to Grandma. This was love, simple and pure.

I saw that Page's condition, for all the grief it brings, is in one sense a remarkable and precious gift. For among the many things my brother was born without is the capacity for insincerity. He cannot show what he does not feel, nor can he suppress urgent emotion. Inside him is a clear channel straight to the center of his soul. As I stood next to him, consumed by his expression of unselfish love, I stopped wondering why Page could not be more like me. At that moment, I wanted to be more like him.

We kissed Grandma, one by one, and slowly filed out of the room. I was the last to leave. "Bye, Grandma," I said. As I turned to look at her one last time, I noticed her lips come together, as if she was trying to speak. Somehow, if for an instant, she mustered the strength to say good-bye. That's when I knew Page had reached her.

That afternoon by Grandma's deathbed, when none of us knew what to say, my speechless brother had said it all. 🦢

A Good Rest

WHEN MY husband was away at basic training, my four-year-old daughter and I stayed with my sister. Since my daughter already called me Mommy, she started calling her aunt Mom—the way her six-year-old cousin did. One day, someone called. I picked up the extension and overheard the person ask my daughter if her daddy was home.

She said, "No, he's in the Army."

"Is your mom home?" he asked.

"Yes, but she's asleep with Uncle Danny."

Tonya Aleisawi

The Ugliest Cat in the World

BY PENNY PORTER

March 1993

THE FIRST time I ever saw Smoky, she was on fire. My three children and I had arrived at the dump outside our Arizona desert town to throw out the weekly trash. As we approached the pit, which was smoldering, we heard the most mournful cries of a cat entombed in the smoking rubble.

Suddenly a large cardboard box, which had been wired shut, burst into flames and exploded. With a long, piercing meow, the animal imprisoned within shot into the air like a flaming rocket and dropped into the ash-filled crater.

"Mommy, do something!" three-year-old Jaymee cried as she and Becky, six, leaned over the smoking hole.

"It can't possibly be alive," Scott, 16, said. But the ashes moved, and a tiny kitten, charred almost beyond recognition, miraculously struggled to the surface and crawled toward us in agony. "I'll get her!" Scott yelled. As he wrapped the kitten in my bandanna, I wondered why it didn't cry from the added pain. Later we learned we had heard its last meow only moments before.

Back at our ranch, we were doctoring the kitten when my husband, Bill, came in, weary from a long day of fence-mending. When he saw our patient, that familiar "Oh no, not again!" look crossed his face. This wasn't the first time we had greeted him with an injured animal. Though Bill always grumbled, he couldn't bear to see any living creature suffer. So he helped by building perches, pens and splints for the skunks, rabbits and birds we brought home. This was different, however. This was a cat. And Bill, very definitely, did not like cats.

What's more, this was no ordinary cat. Where fur had been, blisters and a sticky black gum remained. Her ears were gone. Her tail was cooked to the bone. Gone were the claws that would have snatched some unsuspecting mouse. Gone were the little paw pads that would have left telltale tracks on our car. Nothing that resembled a cat was left—except for two huge cobalt-blue eyes begging for help. What could we do?

Suddenly I remembered our aloe vera plant, and its supposed healing power on burns. So we peeled the leaves, swathed the kitten in slimy aloe strips and gauze bandages, and placed her in Jaymee's Easter basket. All we could see was her tiny face, like a butterfly waiting to emerge from a cocoon.

Her tongue was severely burned, and the inside of her mouth was so blistered that she couldn't lap, so we fed her fluids with an eyedropper. After a while, she began eating by herself. We named her Smoky.

Three weeks later, we coated Smoky with a salve that turned her body a curious shade of green. Her tail dropped off. Not a hair remained. And the children and I adored her.

Bill didn't. And Smoky despised him. The reason: Bill was a pipe smoker armed with matches and butane lighters. When he lit up, Smoky panicked, knocking over cups and lamps before fleeing into the open air duct in the spare bedroom.

In time, Smoky became more tolerant. She'd lie on the sofa and glare at Bill as he puffed away. One day he looked at me and chuckled, "Damn cat makes me feel guilty."

As Smoky's health improved, we marveled at her patience with the girls, who dressed her in doll clothes and bonnets so the "no ears" wouldn't show.

Then they held her up to the mirror so she could see "how pretty" she was.

By the end of her first year, Smoky resembled a well-used welding glove. Scott was famous among his friends for owning the ugliest pet in the county—probably, the world.

Smoky longed to play outside where the sounds of birds, chickens and chipmunks tempted her. When it was time to feed our outdoor pets, including our Mexican wolf, the occasional skunks and assorted lizards, she sat inside, spellbound, with her nose pressed against the window. It was the barn cats, however, that caused her tiny body to tremble with eagerness. But since she had no claws for protection, we couldn't let her go outside unwatched.

Occasionally we took Smoky on the porch when other animals weren't around. If she was lucky an unsuspecting beetle or June bug would make the mistake of strolling across the concrete. Smoky would stalk, bat and toss the bug until it flipped onto its back, where, one hopes, it died of fright before she ate it.

Slowly, oddly, Bill became the one she cared for the most. And before long, I noticed a change in him. He rarely smoked in the house now, and one winter night, to my astonishment, I found him sitting in his chair with the leathery little cat curled up on his lap. Before I could comment, he mumbled a curt "She's probably cold—no fur you know." But Smoky, I re-minded myself, liked being cold. Didn't she sleep in front of air ducts and on the cold brick floor? Perhaps Bill was starting to like this strange-looking animal just a bit.

Not everyone shared our feelings for Smoky, espe-cially those who had never seen her. Rumors reached a group of self-appointed animal protectors, and one day one of them arrived at our door.

"I've had numerous calls and letters," the woman said. "All these dear souls are concerned about a poor little burned-up cat you have in your house. They say," her voice dropped an octave, "she's suffering." Per-haps it should be put out of its misery?

I was furious. Bill was even more so. "Burned she was," he said, "but suffering? Look for yourself."

"Here kitty," I called. No Smoky. "She's probably hiding," I said, but our guest didn't answer. When I turned and looked at her, the woman's skin was gray, her mouth hung open and two fingers pointed.

Magnified tenfold in all her naked splendor, Smoky glowered at the visitor from her hiding place behind our 150-gallon aquarium. The effect was awe-some. Instead of the "poor little burned-up suffering creature" the woman had expected to see, a veritable tyrannosaurus Smoky leered at her through the green aquatic maze. Her open jaws exposed saberlike fangs that glinted menacingly in the neon light. Moments later the woman was gone—smiling now, a little em-barrassed and greatly relieved.

During Smoky's second year, a miraculous thing happened. She began growing fur. Tiny white hairs, softer and finer than the down on a chick, gradually grew over three inches long, transforming our ugly little cat into a wispy puff of smoke.

Bill continued to enjoy her company, though the two made an incongruous pair—the big weather-worn rancher driving around with an unlit pipe clenched between his teeth, accompanied by the tiny white ball of fluff. When he got out of the truck to check the cat-tle, he left the air conditioner on for her comfort. Or he picked her up and held her against his denim jacket.

Smoky was three years old on the day she went with Bill to look for a missing calf. Searching for hours, he would leave the truck door open when he got out to look. The pastures were parched and crisp with dried grasses and tumbleweed. A storm loomed on the horizon, and still no calf. Discouraged, without thinking, Bill reached into his pocket for his lighter and spun the wheel. A spark shot to the ground and, in seconds, the weeds were on fire.

Frantic, Bill didn't think about the cat. Only after the fire was under control and the calf found did he re-turn home and remember. "Smoky!" he cried. "She must have jumped out of the truck! Did she come home?"

No. And we knew she'd never find her way home

from two miles away. To make matters worse, it had started to rain—so hard we couldn't go out to look for her.

Bill was distraught, blaming himself. We spent the next day searching, knowing she'd be helpless against predators. It was no use.

TWO WEEKS later Smoky still wasn't home. We assumed she was dead by now, for the rainy season had begun, and the hawks, wolves and coyotes had families to feed.

Then came the biggest rainstorm our region had had in 50 years. By morning, flood waters stretched for miles, marooning wildlife and cattle on scattered islands of higher ground. Frightened rabbits, raccoons, squirrels and desert rats waited for the water to subside, while Bill and Scott waded knee-deep, carrying bawling calves back to their mamas and safety.

The girls and I were watching intently when suddenly Jaymee shouted, "Daddy! There's a poor little rabbit over there. Can you get it?"

Bill waded to the spot where the animal lay, but when he reached out to help the tiny creature, it seemed to shrink back in fear. "I don't believe it," Bill cried. "It's Smoky!" His voice broke. "Little Smoky!"

My eyes ached with tears when that pathetic little cat crawled into the outstretched hands of the man she had grown to love. He pressed her shivering body to his chest, talked to her softly and gently wiped the mud from her face. All the while her blue eyes fastened on his with unspoken understanding. He was forgiven.

Smoky came home again. The patience she showed us as we shampooed her astounded us. We fed her scrambled eggs and ice cream, and to our joy she seemed to get well.

But Smoky had never really been strong. One morning when she was barely four years old, we found her limp in Bill's chair. Her heart had simply stopped.

As I wrapped her body in one of Bill's red neckerchiefs and placed her in a child's shoe box, I thought of the many things Smoky had taught us about trust, affection and struggling against the odds when everything says you can't win. She reminded us that it's not what's outside that counts—it's what's inside, deep in our hearts.

That's why Smoky will always be in my heart. And why, to me, she'll always be the most beautiful cat in the world. 🦢

Glass Half Full

I HAVE long been teased about my large nose, and I sought some reassurance from a friend.

"Is it really that big?" I asked.

"No, your nose isn't big," he replied. "It's just that your face is too far back." *Tony Murray*

My Fourteenth Summer

BY W. W. MEADE

July 1998

O NE EVENING I sat in Miami's Pro Player Stadium watching a baseball game between the Florida Marlins and the New York Mets. During the seventh-inning stretch. I noticed a teenage boy and his father one row in front of me. The father was a Mets fan, by the looks of his cap; his son's bore the Marlins' logo.

The father began ribbing his son about the Marlins, who were losing. The son's responses grew increasingly sharp. Finally, with the Marlins hopelessly behind, the boy turned to his father in a full-bore adolescent snarl. "I hate you!" he said. "You know that!" He spat the words as though they tasted as bad in his mouth as they sounded. Then he got up and took the steps two at a time toward the grandstand.

His father shook his head

In a moment he stood and squeezed out of his row of seats, looking both angry and bereft. Our eyes met. "Kids!" he said, as though that explained everything.

I sympathized—after all, I was a father now. But I knew how father *and* son felt. There was a time when I, too, had turned on the man who loved me most.

MY FATHER was a country doctor who raised Hereford cattle on our farm in southern Indiana. A white four-board fence around the property had to be scraped and painted every three years. That was to be my job the summer after my freshman year in high school. If that wasn't bad enough news, one June day my dad decided I should extend the fence.

We were sitting at the edge of the south pasture, my father thoughtfully whittling a piece of wood, as he often did. He took off his Stetson and wiped his forehead. Then he pointed to a stand of hemlocks 300 yards away. "From here to there—that's where we want our fence," he said. "Figure about 110 holes, three feet deep. Keep the digger's blades sharp and you can probably dig eight or ten a day."

In a tight voice I said I didn't see how I could

finish that with all the other stuff I had to do. Besides, I'd planned a little softball and fishing. "Why don't we borrow a power auger?" I suggested.

"Power augers don't learn anything from work. And we want our fence to teach us a thing or two," he replied, slapping me on the back.

I flinched to show my resentment. What made me especially mad was the way he said "our" fence. The project was his, I told him. I was just the labor. Dad shook his head with an exasperated expression, then went back to his piece of wood.

I admired a lot about my dad, and I tried to remember those things when I felt mad at him. Once, when I'd been along on one of his house calls, I watched him tell a sick farm woman she was going to be all right before he left or he wasn't leaving. He held her hand and told her stories. He got her to laugh and then he got her out of bed. She said "Why, Doc, I do feel better."

I asked him later how he knew she would get better. "I didn't," he said. "But if you don't push too hard and you keep their morale up, most patients will get things fixed up themselves." I wanted to ask why he didn't treat his own family that way, but I thought better of it.

IF I wanted to be by myself, I would retreat to a river birch by the stream that fed our pond. It forked at ground level, and I'd wedge my back up against one trunk and my feet against the other. Then I would look at the sky or read or pretend.

That summer I hadn't had much time for my tree. One evening as my father and I walked past it, he said, "I remember you scrunchin' into that tree when you were a little kid."

"I don't," I said sullenly.

He looked at me sharply. "What's got into you?" he said.

Amazingly, I heard myself say, "What the hell do you care?" Then I ran off to the barn. Sitting in the tack room, I tried not to cry.

My father opened the door and sat opposite me. Finally I met his gaze.

"It's not a good idea to doctor your own family," he said. "But I guess I need to do that for you right now." He leaned forward. "Let's see. You feel strange in your own body, like it doesn't work the same way it always had. You think no one else is like you. And you think I'm too hard on you and don't appreciate what you do around here. You even wonder how you got into a family as dull as ours."

I was astonished that he knew my most treacherous night thoughts.

"The thing is, your body is changing," he continued. "And that changes your entire self. You've got a lot more male hormones in your blood. And,

Son, there's not a man in this world who could handle what that does to you when you're fourteen."

I didn't know what to say. I knew I didn't like whatever was happening to me. For months I'd felt out of touch with everything. I was irritable and restless and sad for no reason. And because I couldn't talk about it, I began to feel really isolated.

"One of the things that'll help you," my dad said after a while, "is work. Hard work."

As soon as he said that, I suspected it was a ploy to keep me busy doing chores. Anger came suddenly. "Fine," I said in the rudest voice I could manage. Then I stormed out.

WHEN MY father said work he meant *work*. I dug post holes every morning, slamming that digger into the ground until I had tough calluses on my hands.

One morning I helped my father patch the barn roof. We worked in silence. In the careful way my father worked, I could see how he felt about himself, the barn, the whole farm. I was sure he didn't know what it was like to be on the outside looking in.

Just then, he looked at me and said, "You *aren't* alone you know."

Startled, I stared at him, squatting above me with the tar bucket in his hand. How could he possibly know what I'd been thinking?

"Think about this," he said. "If you drew a line

from your feet down the side of our barn to the earth and followed it any which way, it would touch every living thing in the world. So you're never alone. No one is."

I started to argue, but the notion of being connected to all of life made me feel so good that I let my thoughts quiet down.

As I worked through the summer, I began to notice my shoulders getting bigger. I was able to do more work, and I even started paying some attention to doing it well. I had hated hole-digging, but it seemed to release some knot inside me, as if the anger I felt went driving into the earth. Slowly I started to feel I could get through this rotten time.

One day near the end of the summer, I got rid of a lot of junk from my younger days. Afterward I went to sit in my tree as a kind of last visit to the world of my boyhood. I had to scuttle up eight feet to get space enough for my body. As I stretched out, I could feel the trunk beneath my feet weakening. Something had gotten at it—ants, maybe, or just plain age.

I pushed harder. Finally, the trunk gave way and fell to the ground. Then I cut up my tree for firewood.

THE AFTERNOON I finished the fence, I found my father sitting on a granite outcrop in the south pasture. "You thinking about how long this grass is going to hold out with rain?" I asked.

"Yes," he said. "How long you think we got?"

"Another week. Easy."

He turned and looked me deep in the eyes. Of course I wasn't really talking about the pasture as much as I was trying to find out if my opinion mattered to him. After a while he said, "You could be right." He paused and added, "You did a fine job on our fence."

"Thanks," I said almost overwhelmed by the force of his approval.

"You know," he said, "you're going to turn out to be one hell of a man. But just because you're getting grown up doesn't mean you have to leave behind everything you liked when you were a boy."

I knew he was thinking about my tree. He reached into his jacket pocket and pulled out a piece of wood the size of a deck of cards. "I made this for you," he said.

It was a piece of the heartwood from the river birch. He had carved it so the tree appeared again, tall and strong. Beneath were the words "Our Tree."

LEAVING THE Miami stadium that day, I saw the man and the boy walking toward the parking lot. The man's arm rested comfortably on his son's shoulder. I didn't know how they'd made their peace, but it seemed worth acknowledging. As I passed, I tipped my cap—to them, and to my memories of the past. 🦢

Mother Courage

BY LINDA KRAMER JENNING

June 2009

EVERY MORNING, Becky Ziegel gets anxious. Just before ten, sitting at her kitchen counter with a cup of coffee, she tries to concentrate on the day ahead. But her eyes keep drifting to the cell phone at her elbow. Where is the text message from Ty?

"If I don't hear from him," she says, "it's panic time. I'll call him, and if he doesn't answer, I'm in my car. I'll drive over to his house with my heart pounding so hard, I can feel it in my neck."

Now a chiming sound signals a new message, and

Becky's shoulders relax as she reads it: "Brain and bodily functions seem to be working as 'normally' as possible." She can head upstairs to her sewing room knowing that her son made it through another night.

"I'd be dead if my parents weren't within driving distance," says Tyler Ziegel, who is 26 and lives in his own place about ten miles from his family's home in Metamora, Illinois. Ty, a former Marine, is officially retired from the military, with disability compensation for the massive injuries he sustained in a suicide bombing in western Iraq. He lost part of his left arm and right hand, most of his face, and a piece of his brain. Today, he has recovered enough to function without constant care, but seizures and other health problems have sent him to the ER four times in recent months.

In 2006, two years after he was wounded, Ty wed his hometown sweetheart, Renee Kline, to whom he had proposed between his two deployments to Iraq. The event drew worldwide media attention. But the marriage unraveled, and the couple divorced after a year. ("We grew apart, went our own ways," says Ty, with practical detachment.) Since then, Becky, like thousands of mothers of disabled vets, has been her son's main caregiver. While Ty credits his whole family and his friends for rallying around him, he singles her out. "My mom has been awesome," he says. "She's been there for me through everything."

"I unloaded him, and now he's back," Becky says,

laughing. She drives him to appointments at the Veterans Affairs clinic in nearby Peoria and the VA hospital more than two hours away in Danville. She makes sure he eats well and takes his medications. She helps him with the housecleaning and bill paying. And, of course, she checks every morning that her son is still breathing.

"I'm the mom," she says. "This is what I do."

BECKY IS 49 and the mother of two Marines, both of whom joined up after high school. Ty shipped out to Iraq for his second tour in the summer of 2004, shortly after his little brother, Zach, left for boot camp. With both boys gone, Becky admits, she "did the happy dance." She and her husband, Jeff, 56, a heavy-equipment operator, finally had an empty nest. "I was thinking, They're grown; they don't need me anymore. Who do I want to be?" She considered taking some college classes; she planned to visit friends she hadn't seen in years.

One day in December, Ty was on patrol in Anbar province when an Iraqi insurgent detonated a carload of explosives beside the convoy's troop truck. Of the seven men on board, Ty took the hardest hit. A buddy pulled him out and smothered the flames. Ty was evacuated to a military hospital at Balad Air Base, where surgeons worked to save his life.

Becky was getting ready to wrap Christmas

presents when a Marine officer called with the news. When Jeff handed her the phone, she didn't cry but pumped the officer for information. He could offer little more than a sketchy description of the attack and Ty's injuries. The house soon filled with relatives and friends.

From Balad, Ty was flown 17 hours to Brooke Army Medical Center in San Antonio, Texas. The Fisher House Foundation—a national nonprofit that aids and temporarily houses the families of wounded soldiers—arranged for plane tickets for Becky and Jeff, along with Ty's fiancée, Renee, and Zach, who was just home on leave. They got to Brooke on Christmas Eve.

A neurologist filled them in on Ty's condition. Surgeons at Balad had removed the shrapnel-pierced part of his left frontal lobe. It was too soon to know if his mental capability or his personality would be altered, if he would be paralyzed, if he'd even wake up at all. Everything above his waist was severely burned. "They really didn't expect him to make it," says Becky.

When the family entered Ty's room, they found him wrapped in bandages with a tube protruding from his head. "We couldn't see his face," Becky recalls. "But his legs poked out, and I could see the crossed-rifles tattoo. That's how I knew it was Ty."

Ty endured multiple surgeries. His left forearm and three fingers on his right hand were amputated—the thumb, index, and middle. He was kept sedated most of the time. Then, after several weeks, the doctors removed the bandages. "Bits of his face looked like him, only burnt," Becky says. "I can't describe the color—charcoal, brown. No ears, no nose."

Later operations, including one that used a muscle from Ty's back to cover the exposed part of his brain, changed his appearance even more. For a few months, he wore a lacrosse helmet to protect the area, until a molded prosthetic was inserted and his skull stitched closed. "He went through so many stages of healing that I just grew into how he looked," says Becky, who says she was more concerned with Ty's emotional well-being than his physical appearance.

After Ty survived the first critical weeks, his father and brother flew back to Metamora. Becky and Renee stayed behind, moving into a suite at the local Fisher House. The women rotated shifts at Ty's bedside. They fed him and helped him shower. They stretched his remaining two fingers—both badly burned—to increase their range of motion. "I remember days I'd think, I can't walk in that room and put on a happy face," Becky says. "I don't know how I did it. I just did. My kid."

Ty, his perception fogged by sedatives and painkillers, only gradually became aware of his disfigurement. Following the doctors' advice, Becky didn't volunteer details but waited for him to ask. One day, when he wanted to blow his nose, Ty remarked, "As bad as I was burned, I'm surprised I still have a nose." Then he saw the look in his mother's eyes. "No nose?" he said. "I must really look like an alien."

Once, as they entered a treatment room, Becky wasn't able to block her son from a full-length mirror. It was the first time he got a good look at himself. Remarkably, he seemed more curious than horrified. As Ty healed, he and Becky made forays into San Antonio to shop and eat, and Becky would stare down gawkers. If Ty was bothered by the attention, he rarely let it show.

That May, Jeff came to visit and brought Becky a ring with three diamonds—past, present, and future—to celebrate their 25th wedding anniversary. They strolled on San Antonio's River Walk and took in the sights. Becky had been living at Fisher House for five months. One more anniversary would come and go before she got back home.

SHE'D NEVER spent much time away from the patch of country outside Peoria where she was raised. The eldest of seven children whose parents separated when she was a teenager, Becky learned to be independent and hardworking and to put others first. She waited on tables during high school and later took a courier job at the hospital where her mother was a registered nurse. She married Jeff at 20, and they bought her grandparents' old house, which is still her home.

"I never could have imagined living somewhere else and not having family and friends around," she says. But her 19 months in San Antonio opened up "the little box" of her world. "Now I can go anywhere and make friends and find family."

Terri Fulkerson, whose daughter was also in the burn unit at Brooke, would sit with Becky in the gazebo outside Fisher House after long days at the hospital and "talk mom." "That girl could find humor in a rock," says Terri. "She has a way of pulling laughter out of someone even if their dreams are crashing down around them."

Becky also became expert at dealing with medical personnel. "I would never have dreamed of arguing with a neurosurgeon before," she says. She supported the decision to transplant Ty's big toe to his right hand to create a thumb, though doctors warned it might not work (it did), and stood by when they fitted him with a prosthesis for his left forearm and hand. When he became an outpatient and moved in with Becky and Renee at Fisher House, Becky watched therapists retrain him in skills such as making a bed and loading a dishwasher.

Becky was delighted to see Ty moving toward independence. Aside from headaches, he showed no signs of lasting brain damage. He was as blunt and stubborn as ever and had inherited his mother's wry humor: He regularly rattled young medics by pointing to himself and warning, "Don't smoke while shining your boots."

With Ty making progress, Becky took some time for herself. She walked for miles on a track near the hospital. On the "your-son-getting-blown-up diet," she shed 60 pounds. She let her short blond perm grow shoulder-length and dyed it auburn.

"I was finding me," Becky recalls. "I felt better about myself." She even began doing public speaking to raise support for Fisher House. Then finally, in July 2006, Ty and Becky headed home.

AFTER TY got married, his mother enrolled in the college courses she'd looked forward to for so long. Even after Ty and Renee separated, Becky held on to her new freedom. Ty stayed in the white clapboard bungalow he'd lived in with his wife. He'd been diagnosed with post-traumatic stress disorder, but medication helped lessen his anxiety. He spent his time roughhousing with his boxer pup, tinkering with his truck and noodling on his guitar (he'd learned to drive again and to pick out tunes). At night, he'd hit the local bars with friends and even dated a bit.

Then he was struck with a severe sinus infection, which led to two ER visits. The second time, it was the day after Becky had had surgery for a tear in her shoulder. She called Ty and got no answer; Jeff went to check on him and found him dangerously dehydrated. Ty was rushed to the hospital. Jeff suffered a suspected heart attack and landed in the ER himself.

Zach sent an e-mail to Becky from Iraq, where he'd been deployed the previous fall: "What was God thinking? Why does all this stuff have to be happening to us?"

Becky typed back, "Because we can handle it."

There'd be more to handle. Becky and Jeff couldn't wake Ty up at his home one evening; at the hospital, he was diagnosed with seizures—a previously undetected result of his brain injury—and prescribed pills to keep them at bay. Yet a few months later, a neighbor found Ty lying semiconscious in his driveway; there was another trip to the ER, where his medication was adjusted.

Becky surfed the Internet researching seizures and has now learned to recognize the warning signals. When Ty began to nod off—a red flag—over breakfast at his grandmother's recently, Becky persuaded him to come home with her. Hours later, he woke up and asked, "Would you feel comfortable taking me to my place?"

"Honestly, I wouldn't," she replied.

Ty complained to Jeff, in mock irritation, "She's holding me hostage." Still, later that night, he allowed, "When I'm at your house, Mom, I know everything will be fine."

AT DINNERTIME, Becky and Jeff are hanging out, waiting for a pizza delivery. The phone rings: Ty asking how to defrost a hot dog bun. Chuckling, Becky imparts some motherly wisdom.

Sometimes—not often—she feels almost overwhelmed by the hand life has dealt her, and she worries. "What if something happens? What if I don't get there in time? It scares the hell out of me." She finds comfort, though, in her circle of loved ones and her "second family" of wounded vets and their parents. She tries not to dwell on what she can't change.

"Ty asked me once if I was angry about what happened to him," Becky says. "But who would I be angry at? The bomber? He's dead. Ty? I'm proud of him. I couldn't pick anybody to be angry at, so I wasn't angry."

Her studies on hold, job offers let go, Becky fully expects to pick up where she left off sometime in the future. She imagines the day when Ty will need her less, even marry again. "The woman who ends up with him is going to be lucky," she says. "I can't wait till he has his own kids.

"I don't expect to be at Ty's beck and call for the rest of my life," she adds, curling up on the sofa where her son often sleeps. "But you're never done being the mom."

Heroes
Heroes
Heroes
Heroe

An Open Letter to Students

DWIGHT D. EISENHOWER

October 1948

AS PRESIDENT of Columbia University I receive many letters from young people. Mostly they ask a question that could be put like this: Shall I keep on with school, or shall I plunge right off into "life?"

I try to answer each according to the circumstances. But if I could write a general answer, I think I would say:

Dear Jack—or Margaret: You say you wonder if it is worthwhile for you to go on with school. You particularly wonder if it is worthwhile to enter and finish college. The tedium of study, nose buried in books, seems a waste of time compared with a job and the stimulus of productive work. This problem of yours is not a trifling one at all. Your decision will affect your whole life, and I know how deeply it must worry you. It worried me when I was your age.

In a small Kansas town, 40 years ago, a reasonably strong case could be put up in favor of leaving school early. Most of us knew our lives would be spent on the farm, or in one of the local stores, or at the creamery or elevator. The quickest road to practical knowledge was to *do*. That was the way we might have argued—and rightly, if there were no more to successful living than plowing a straight furrow, wrapping a neat package, keeping a machine well oiled.

Fortunately, we came of stock that set the school on the same plane as the home and church. The value of education had been bred into us. Our families stinted themselves to keep us in school a while longer, and most of us worked, and worked hard, to prolong that while.

Today the business of living is far more complex. No one of us can hope to comprehend all its complexity in a lifetime of study. But each day profitably spent in school will help you understand better your own relationship to country and world. If your generation fails to understand that the individual is still the center, the sole reason for the existence of all man-made institutions, then complexity will become chaos.

Consequently, I feel firmly that you should continue your schooling—if you can—right to the end of college. You say you are "not too good at books." I got a moving letter from a young girl halfway through high school. She said that in her studies she seemed to be always trailing. But she concluded: "I still think I can learn to be a good American."

That's the vital point. School, of course, should train you in the two great basic tools of the mind: the use of words and the use of numbers. And school can properly give you a start toward the special skills you may need in a trade, business or profession. But remember: As soon as you enter an occupation, you will be strongly tempted to fall into the routine of it, to become just a part of that occupation, which is just one part of America. In school—from books, from teachers, from fellow students—you can get a view of the whole of America, how it started, how it grew, what it is, what it means. Each day will add breadth to your view and a sharper comprehension of your own role.

I feel sure I am right when I tell you: *To develop fully your own character you must know your country's character.* A plant partakes of the character of the soil in which it grows. You are a plant that is *conscious,* that *thinks.* You must study your soil—which is your country—in order that you may be able to draw its strength up into your own strength.

It will pay you to do so. You will understand your own problems better and solve them more easily if you have studied America's problems and done something toward their solution. You have to look out for yourself *and* your country. Self-interest and patriotism, rightly considered, are not contradictory ideas. They are partners.

The very earth of our country is gradually getting lost to us. One third of the fertile top layer of our soil has already been washed away into rivers and the sea. This must be stopped or someday our country will be too barren to yield us a living. That is one national problem crying for solution.

In our cities there are millions of people who have little between them and hunger except a daily job, which they may lose. They demand more security. If they feel too insecure, their discontent might someday undermine *your* security, no matter how successful you might be in your own working life. That's another problem, and there are innumerable others.

It is dangerous to assume that our country's welfare belongs alone to that mysterious mechanism called "the government." Every time we allow or force the government, because of our own individual or local failures, to take over a question that properly belongs to us, by that much we surrender our individual responsibility—and with it freedom. But the very core of what we mean by Americanism is individual liberty, founded on individual responsibility, equality before the law, and a system of private enterprise that aims to reward according to merit.

Yours is a country of free men and women, where personal liberty is cherished as a fundamental right. But liberty is easily lost; the price of its continued possession is untiring alertness.

Never let yourself be persuaded that any one Great Man, any one leader, is necessary to the salvation of America. When America consists of one *leader* and a population of millions of *followers,* it will no longer be America. Any needless concentration of power is a menace to freedom.

World War II was not won by one man or a few men. It was won by hundreds of thousands and millions of men and women of all ranks. Audacity, initiative, the will to try greatly and stubbornly characterized them. Great numbers of them, if for only a few minutes in some desperate crisis of battle, were leaders.

You will find it so in the fields of peace. America at work is not just a few Great Men at the head of government, of corporation or of labor unions. It is millions and millions of men and women who on farms and in factories and in stores, offices and homes are leading this country—and the world—toward better and better ways of doing and making things.

We have the world's best machines because we

ourselves are not machines; because we have embraced the liberty of thinking for ourselves, imagining for ourselves, and acting for ourselves out of our own energies and inspirations. Our true strength is not in our machines, splendid as they are, but in the inquisitive, inventive, indomitable souls of our people.

To be that kind of soul is open to every American boy and girl; *and it is the one kind of career that the nation cannot live without.* To be a good American—worthy of the heritage that is yours, eager to pass it on enhanced and enriched—is a lifetime career, stimulating, sometimes exhausting, always satisfying.

Start on it now; take part in America's affairs while you are still a student. "Let no man despise thy youth," Paul the Apostle said to Timothy. These words apply to you as an American. Loyalty to principle, readiness to give of one's talents to the common good, acceptance of responsibility—in home, neighborhood, school: these are the measure of a good American, not his age in years. Alexander Hamilton—General Washington's aide in war, President Washington's Secretary of the Treasury in peace—was speaking before applauding crowds of his fellow New Yorkers on the political problems of the American Revolution when he was only 17 years old and still a student in King's College, now Columbia University. The same stuff of which he was made is in you.

Above all, while still in school, try to learn the

"why" of your country. To assure each citizen his inalienable right to life, liberty and the pursuit of happiness: that was the "why" for its continued existence. What that means to you personally, what you must do toward its fulfillment, cannot be answered completely in a letter. But I repeat that the answer can be found in your school, if you seek it deliberately and conscientiously. And need neither genius nor vast learning for its comprehension.

To be a good American is essentially nothing more than being a good member of your community, helping those who need your help, striving for a sympathetic understanding of those who oppose you, doing each new day's job a little better than the previous day's, placing the common good before personal profit. The American Republic was born to assure you the dignity and rights of a human individual. If the dignity and rights of your fellow men guide your daily conduct of life, you will be a good American. 🕊

Animal Magnetism

I WAS looking through my closet for something to wear, but nothing was calling out to me. So I sought my three-year-old's opinion.

"What do you think I should change into?" I asked.

He thought awhile before replying, "A butterfly."

Lynn Sherlock

Three Days to See

March 1933

FROM *The Atlantic Monthly*

I HAVE OFTEN thought it would be a blessing if each human being were stricken blind and deaf for a few days at some time during his early adult life. Darkness would make him more appreciative of sight; silence would teach him the joys of sound.

Now and then I have tested my seeing friends to discover what they see. Recently I asked a friend, who had just returned from a long walk in the woods, what she had observed. "Nothing in particular," she replied.

How was it possible, I asked myself, to walk for

an hour through the woods and see nothing worthy of note? I who cannot see find hundreds of things to interest me through mere touch. I feel the delicate symmetry of a leaf. I pass my hands lovingly about the smooth skin of a silver birch, or the rough, shaggy bark of a pine. In spring I touch the branches of trees hopefully in search of a bud, the first sign of awakening Nature after her winter's sleep. Occasionally, if I am very fortunate, I place my hand gently on a small tree and feel the happy quiver of a bird in full song.

At times my heart cries out with longing to see all these things. If I can get so much pleasure from mere touch, how much more beauty must be revealed by sight. And I have imagined what I should most like to see if I were given the use of my eyes, say, for just three days.

I should divide the period into three parts. On the first day, I should want to see the people whose kindness and companionship have made my life worth living. I do not know what it is to see into the heart of a friend through that "window of the soul," the eye. I can only "see" through my fingertips the outline of a face. I can detect laughter, sorrow and many other obvious emotions. I know my friends from the feel of their faces.

How much easier, how much more satisfying it is for you who can see to grasp quickly the essential qualities of another person by watching the subtleties of expression, the quiver of a muscle, the flutter of a hand. But does it ever occur to you to use your sight to see into the inner nature of a friend? Do not most of you seeing people grasp casually the outward features of a face and let it go at that?

For instance, can you describe accurately the faces of five good friends? As an experiment, I have questioned husbands about the color of their wives' eyes, and often they express embarrassed confusion and admit that they do not know.

Oh, the things that I should see if I had the power of sight for just three days!

THE FIRST day would be a busy one. I should call to me all my dear friends and look long into their faces, imprinting upon my mind the outward evidences of the beauty that is within them. I should let my eyes rest, too, on the face of a baby, so that I could catch a vision of the eager, innocent beauty which precedes the individual's consciousness of the conflicts which life develops. I should like to see the books which have been read to me, and which have revealed to me the deepest channels of human life. And I should like to look into the loyal, trusting eyes of my dogs, the little Scottie and the stalwart Great Dane.

In the afternoon I should take a long walk in the woods and intoxicate my eyes on the beauties of the world of Nature. And I should pray for the glory of a colorful sunset. That night, I think, I should not be able to sleep.

THE NEXT day I should arise with the dawn and see the thrilling miracle by which night is transformed into day. I should behold with awe the magnificent panorama of light with which the sun awakens the sleeping earth. This day I should devote to a hasty glimpse of the world, past and present. I should want to see the pageant of man's progress, and so I should go to the museums. There my eyes would see the condensed history of the earth—animals and the races of men pictured in their native environment; gigantic carcasses of dinosaurs and mastodons which roamed the earth before man appeared, with his tiny stature and powerful brain, to conquer the animal kingdom.

My next stop would be the Museum of Art. I know well through my hands the sculptured gods and goddesses of the ancient Nile land. I have felt copies of Parthenon friezes, and I have sensed the rhythmic beauty of charging Athenian warriors. The gnarled, bearded features of Homer are dear to me, for he, too, knew blindness.

So on this, my second day, I should try to probe into the soul of man through his art. The things I knew through touch I should now see. More splendid still, the whole magnificent world of painting would be opened to me. I should be able to get only a superficial impression. Artists tell me that for a deep and true appreciation of art one must educate the eye. One must learn through experience to weigh the merits of line, of composition, of form and color. If I had eyes, how happily would I embark on so fascinating a study!

The evening of my second day I should spend at a theater or at the movies. How I should like to see the fascinating figure of Hamlet, or the gusty Falstaff amid colorful Elizabethan trappings! I cannot enjoy the beauty of rhythmic movement except in a sphere restricted to the touch of my hands. I can vision only dimly the grace of a Pavlova, although I know something of the delight of rhythm, for often I can sense the beat of music as it vibrates through the floor. I can well imagine that cadenced motion must be one of the most pleasing sights in the world. I have been able to gather something of this by tracing with my fingers the lines in sculptured marble; if this static grace can be so lovely, how much more acute must be the thrill of seeing grace in motion.

THE FOLLOWING morning, I should again greet the dawn, anxious to discover new delights, new revelations of beauty. Today, this third day, I shall spend in the workaday world, amid the haunts of men going about the business of life. The city becomes my destination.

First, I stand at a busy corner, merely looking at

people, trying by sight of them to understand some-thing of their daily lives. I see smiles, and I am happy. I see serious determination, and I am proud. I see suf-fering, and I am compassionate.

I stroll down Fifth Avenue. I throw my eyes out of focus, so that I see no particular object but only a seething kaleidoscope of color. I am certain that the colors of women's dresses moving in a throng must be a gorgeous spectacle of which I should never tire. But perhaps if I had sight I should be like most other women—too interested in styles to give much atten-tion to the splendor of color in the mass.

From Fifth Avenue I make a tour of the city—to the slums, to factories, to parks where children play. I take a stay-at-home trip abroad by visiting the for-eign quarters. Always my eyes are open wide to all the sights of both happiness and misery so that I may probe deep and add to my understanding of how peo-ple work and live.

My third day of sight is drawing to an end. Perhaps there are many serious pursuits to which I should de-vote the few remaining hours, but I am afraid that on the evening of that last day I should again run away to the theater, to a hilariously funny play, so that I might appreciate the overtones of comedy in the hu-man spirit.

At midnight permanent night would close in on me again. Naturally in those three short days I should not have seen all I wanted to see. Only when darkness had again descended upon me should I realize how much I had left unseen.

Perhaps this short outline does not agree with the program you might set for yourself if you knew that you were about to be stricken blind. I am, however, sure that if you faced that fate you would use your eyes as never before. Everything you saw would become dear to you. Your eyes would touch and embrace every object that came within your range of vision. Then, at last, you would really see, and a new world of beauty would open itself before you.

I WHO am blind can give one hint to those who see: Use your eyes as if tomorrow you would be stricken blind. And the same method can be applied to the other senses. Hear the music of voices, the song of a bird, the mighty strains of an orchestra, as if you would be stricken deaf tomorrow. Touch each object as if tomorrow your tactile sense would fail. Smell the perfume of flowers, taste with relish each morsel, as if tomorrow you could never smell and taste again. Make the most of every sense; glory in all the facets of pleasure and beauty which the world reveals to you through the several means of contact which Nature provides. But of all the senses, I am sure that sight must be the most delightful.

How America Can Make Brotherhood Work

BY BILL BRADLEY

1997

ALOT OF what I know about racism and about whites and blacks getting along I learned growing up in Crystal City, Missouri, a multi-racial, one-stop-light town on the banks of the Mississippi. My father, a local banker, used to say, "The color of your skin doesn't predict whether you'll save your money or pay your bills."

I remember, as an 11-year-old Little Leaguer, staying in a run-down hotel in Joplin because better hotels wouldn't take our black players. When I was a teenage player in the American Legion baseball league, my team was refused restaurant service because our catcher and left fielder were black.

After I left Crystal City and finished Princeton and Oxford universities, I played professional basketball for the New York Knicks. Over the years since then, I wish I had a hundred dollars for every time someone, usually a white person, has asked me, "What was it like to play on the Knicks?"

"What was it like? What do you mean?"

"Well, you know—with guys from such different backgrounds and interests."

"You mean, they were black?"

"Well, yes," they'd say. "What was it like?"

"Listen," I'd answer, "traveling with my team on the road in America was one of the most enlightening experiences of my life."

Enjoying warm friendships with black teammates—seeing the powerful role of family in their lives and the strength of each one's individuality—I also began to understand the distrusts and suspicions they had.

I came to know the meaning of certain looks and certain cues. I sensed the tension of always being on guard, never totally relaxing. I felt the pain of racial arrogance directed my way. And I realized how much I will never know about what it is to be black in America.

AFTER MY career with the Knicks, I revived an old dream of mine: to become a United States Senator. I first had that dream in the summer of 1964 when, as a college intern on Capitol Hill, I stood in a corner of the Senate gallery and watched the passage of the civil-rights bill. It would desegregate the hotels and restaurants of Jim Crow America. I realized that something had happened that evening to make this country a better place for everybody.

In 1978 I was elected to the Senate from New Jersey. During my terms, although poverty and violence persisted, I witnessed the dismantlement of the legal architecture of segregation and a rise in the fortunes of Americans of all races. Roughly a third of black American families, for example, can now be characterized as middle class. Latino men imbued with the work ethic have the highest labor-force participation rate in the country. Asian-Americans are models of academic achievement.

But I saw something else evolve, too; something disturbing. Despite our great advances, the races simply don't talk candidly to each other about race. There is no genuine communication about our differences or our shared values—and, even more sadly, a growing lack of interest in even trying.

If we are to have racial healing in America, I'm convinced that the first step is to *engage*—to talk openly and honestly with someone of another race. Yet people of different races often choose to live their lives apart. When they do engage, they don't speak with candor or hear with clarity. The result: Our communication about race is barnacled with code words, inconsequential chatter about sports or the weather—and silence.

But beyond engagement and candor, there must be *action*. The reason our military is one of America's most advanced large institutions in racial terms can be traced to two facts: Clifford Alexander, the first black Secretary of the Army, instituted a promotion system penalizing bias, and a multiracial platoon or company must act together. Their lives depend on each other.

In football, a tackle's race makes no difference; all that counts is whether he blocked the opponent. The race of a basketball player whose last-second shot wins the game is irrelevant; only whether the ball went into the basket matters.

If we are ever to move toward racial harmony in America, we must seize every opportunity for similar cooperation. Only through doing things together—things that have nothing specifically to do with race—will people break down racial barriers. Facing common problems as neighbors or coworkers reduces awkwardness in a way that simple conversation cannot.

It is truly amazing what people working together can do:

• In Alpine, New Jersey, school principal Mat Glowski arranged for 175 eighth-graders from a predominantly black and Hispanic school and other, largely white and Asian schools to sort and package groceries together for the community FoodBank of New Jersey in Hillside. This first step, says Glowski, "demonstrates a hope."

• In tiny Millen, Georgia, the foundation, walls and roof stand where the ashes of a predominantly black Baptist church once lay. The church, burned to the ground in a 1996 hate crime, is being rebuilt by whites and blacks from groups such as the American Jewish Committee and the United Methodists' Volunteers in Mission. "When you're sweating beside others on a work site," says a volunteer, "you get an insight into each other as human beings."

• In Memphis, Tennessee, 25 white and 25 black congregations organized a political-action group and began working together in 1990 on a number of issues, including upgrading schools and trying to stop a highway expansion. In more than 400 meetings between blacks and whites, candor was the rule. When Gerald Taylor, a black leader who was the coalition's organizer, asked white leaders to participate, he told them not to do so "to help poor black folks" but for their own self-interest.

• Walt Michael of Westminster, Maryland, a musician, was troubled that the races were "parked in different camps." So each summer he gets people on "common ground" singing in musical programs at Western Maryland College. For example, Kim, Kellie and Krissy Nichols—a trio of blond, blue-eyed sisters who learned about African-American gospel music singing at the Common Ground concerts—now belt out those songs in black and white churches. The music has proved a powerful bridge between the races.

CAN DEMONSTRATIONS of community overcome the suspicions and bigotries that endure? Over time, I think so. But it will take many acts of individual cooperation, and courage as well.

In 1995 an African-American member of my Senate staff happened to see a Korean-American woman selling refreshments near the Capitol Building during the "Million Man March" on Washington, D.C. At one point a black man walked up to buy a soda.

Another black man, standing nearby with his arms folded like a Praetorian Guard, spoke up. "Not today, my brother!" he said. "Today you buy from a brother, not from her." A few minutes later, another man approached, and the self-appointed guardian said the same.

Finally, a third marcher came by, but he wasn't having any of it. "What do you mean, 'Buy from a brother'?" he said. "Don't you see you're doing the same thing to her that was done to us for two hundred years? I'm buying from her!" And he did.

That man, who saw a fellow human being in that Korean-American woman is a reason to hope that we might one day be able to see beyond skin color or eye shape to the uniqueness of each individual. And he is not alone. Countless men and women of all races share his strength of character.

We can no longer put off the enormous task of racial healing. It is, first, a moral obligation. If our religious faiths teach us that we are our brother's keeper, then we must begin to walk the talk. No longer can our spiritual convictions exist alongside subtle discrimination or a sense of superiority.

Second, it is our obligation as a world leader. Our democratic ideals have the power to stir the world, but they cannot if they are selectively realized at home.

Finally, racial harmony is in our economic self-interest. By the end of the first decade of the next century, only about 60 percent of new American workers will be native-born whites. Clearly, we will all advance together or each of us will be diminished. That is not ideology. It's demographics.

EVERY THANKSGIVING, Americans congregate around a meal and share the joy of friends and family. They laugh, give thanks, nurture each other. Sometimes they even learn from each other.

What America needs now is an annual Sunday of racial healing, in which millions of families of different races sit around common tables and break bread as friends.

It is something every family could do. Blacks would invite whites; whites would invite blacks. A family would invite Asian or Latino neighbors, and vice versa. If enough of us tried it, we would create connections among people now isolated from each other. Through our talk and action, we would get past the initial awkwardness—and restore hope.

Russian writer Leo Tolstoy once observed, "Many people want to change the world; only a few want to change themselves." To achieve racial healing in America, we must start changing ourselves. Making brotherhood work begins with each of us. 🕊

Quotable Quote

IF WE take care of the moments, the years will take care of themselves.   *Maria Edgeworth*

The Night I Met Einstein

BY JEROME WEIDMAN

November 1955

WHEN I was a very young man, just beginning to make my way, I was invited to dine at the home of a distinguished New York philanthropist. After dinner, our hostess led us to an enormous drawing room. Other guests were pouring in, and my eyes beheld two unnerving sights: Servants were arranging small gilt chairs in long, neat rows; and up front, leaning against the wall, were musical instruments.

Apparently I was in for an evening of chamber music.

I USE the phrase "in for" because music meant nothing to me. I am almost tone deaf—only with great effort can I carry the simplest tune, and serious music was to me no more than an arrangement of noises. So I did what I always did when trapped: I sat down, and when the music started, I fixed my face in what I hoped was an expression of intelligent appreciation, closed my ears from the inside and submerged myself in my own completely irrelevant thoughts.

After a while, becoming aware that the people around me were applauding, I concluded it was safe to unplug my ears. At once I heard a gentle but surprisingly penetrating voice on my right: "You are fond of Bach?"

I knew as much about Bach as I know about nuclear fission. But I did know one of the most famous faces in the world, with the renowned shock of untidy white hair and the ever-present pipe between the teeth. I was sitting next to Albert Einstein.

"Well," I said uncomfortably and hesitated. I had been asked a casual question. All I had to do was be equally casual in my reply. But I could see from the look in my neighbor's extraordinary eyes that their owner was not merely going through the perfunctory duties of elementary politeness. Regardless of what value I placed on my part in the verbal exchange, to this man his part in it mattered very much. Above all,

I could feel that this was a man to whom you did not tell a lie, however small.

"I don't know anything about Bach," I said awkwardly. "I've never heard any of his music."

A look of perplexed astonishment washed across Einstein's mobile face.

"You have never heard Bach?"

He made it sound as though I had said I'd never taken a bath.

"It isn't that I don't want to like Bach," I replied hastily. "It's just that I'm tone deaf, or almost tone deaf, and I've never really heard anybody's music."

A look of concern came into the old man's face. "Please," he said abruptly. "You will come with me?"

He stood up and took my arm. I stood up. As he led me across that crowded room, I kept my embarrassed glance fixed on the carpet. A rising murmur of puzzled speculation followed us out into the hall. Einstein paid no attention to it.

Resolutely, he led me upstairs. He obviously knew the house well. On the floor above, he opened the door into a book-lined study, drew me in, and shut the door.

"Now," he said with a small, troubled smile. "You will tell me, please, how long you have felt this way about music?"

"All my life," I said, feeling awful. "I wish you

would go back downstairs and listen, Dr. Einstein. The fact that I don't enjoy it doesn't matter."

Einstein shook his head and scowled, as though I had introduced an irrelevance.

"Tell me, please," he said. "Is there any kind of music that you do like?"

"Well," I answered, "I like songs that have words, and the kind of music where I can follow the tune."

He smiled and nodded, obviously pleased. "You can give me an example, perhaps?"

"Well," I ventured, "almost anything by Bing Crosby."

He nodded again, briskly. "Good!"

HE WENT to a corner of the room, opened a phono-graph, and started pulling out records. I watched him uneasily. At last, he beamed. "Ah!" he said.

He put the record on, and in a moment, the study was filled with the relaxed, lilting strains of Bing Crosby's "When the Blue of the Night Meets the Gold of the Day." Einstein beamed at me and kept time with the stem of his pipe. After three or four phrases, he stopped the phonograph.

"Now," he said. "Will you tell me, please, what you have just heard?"

The simplest answer seemed to be to sing the lines. I did just that, trying desperately to stay in tune and keep my voice from cracking. The expression on Einstein's face was like the sunrise.

"You see!" he cried with delight when I finished. "You do have an ear!"

I mumbled something about this being one of my favorite songs, something I had heard hundreds of times so that it didn't really prove anything.

"Nonsense!" said Einstein. "It proves everything! Do you remember your first arithmetic lesson in school? Suppose, at your very first contact with numbers, your teacher had ordered you to work out a problem in, say, long division or fractions. Could you have done so?"

"No, of course not."

"Precisely!" Einstein made a triumphant wave with his pipe stem. "It would have been impossible, and you would have reacted in panic. You would have closed your mind to long division and fractions. As a result, because of that one small mistake by your teacher, it is possible your whole life you would be denied the beauty of long division and fractions."

The pipe stem went up and out in another wave.

"But on your first day, no teacher would be so foolish. He would start you with elementary things—then, when you had acquired skill with the simplest problems, he would lead you up to long division and to fractions.

"So it is with music." Einstein picked up the Bing

Crosby record. "This simple, charming little song is like simple addition or subtraction. You have mastered it. Now we go on to something more complicated."

HE FOUND another record and set it going. The golden voice of John McCormack singing "The Trumpeter" filled the room. After a few lines, Einstein stopped the record.

"So!" he said. "You will sing that back to me, please?"

I did—with a good deal of self-consciousness but with, for me, a surprising degree of accuracy.

Einstein stared at me with a look on his face that I had seen only once before in my life: on the face of my father as he listened to me deliver the valedictory address at my high school graduation ceremony.

"Excellent!" Einstein remarked when I finished. "Wonderful! Now this!"

"This" turned out to be Caruso in what was to me a completely unrecognizable fragment from *Cavalleria Rusticana,* a one-act opera. Nevertheless, I managed to reproduce an approximation of the sounds the famous tenor had made. Einstein beamed his approval.

Caruso was followed by at least a dozen others. I could not shake my feeling of awe over the way this great man, into whose company I had been thrown by chance, was completely preoccupied by what we were doing, as though I were his sole concern.

We came at last to recordings of music without

words, which I was instructed to reproduce by humming. When I reached for a high note, Einstein's mouth opened, and his head went back as if to help me attain what seemed unattainable. Evidently I came close enough, for he suddenly turned off the phonograph.

"Now, young man," he said, putting his arm through mine. "We are ready for Bach!"

As we returned to our seats in the drawing room, the players were tuning up for a new selection. Einstein smiled and gave me a reassuring pat on the knee.

"Just allow yourself to listen," he whispered. "That is all."

It wasn't really all, of course. Without the effort he had just poured out for a total stranger I would never have heard, as I did that night for the first time in my life, Bach's "Sheep May Safely Graze." I have heard it many times since. I don't think I shall ever tire of it. Because I never listen to it alone. I am sitting beside a small, round man with a shock of untidy white hair, a dead pipe clamped between his teeth and eyes that contain in their extraordinary warmth all the wonder of the world.

When the concert was finished, I added my genuine applause to that of the others.

SUDDENLY OUR hostess confronted us. "I'm so sorry, Dr. Einstein," she said with an icy glare at me, "that you missed so much of the performance."

Einstein and I came hastily to our feet. "I am sorry too," he said. "My young friend here and I, however, were engaged in the greatest activity of which man is capable."

She looked puzzled. "Really?" she said. "And what is that?"

Einstein smiled and put his arm across my shoulders. And he uttered ten words that—for at least one person who is in his endless debt—are his epitaph:

"Opening up yet another fragment of the frontier of beauty."

The Good Samaritans

I GOT talking to a couple at the supermarket and subsequently missed my bus. As I walked home, a car pulled up. Seeing it was my new friends, I jumped in and told them where I lived.

"This was great—thank you," I said when we reached my house. "Do you have much farther to go?"

"Not really," they replied. "We were outside our door when you got in."

Doreen Connor

• • •

"HELLO, MRS. Miller," said the bearded guy behind the counter of the bagel shop.

My husband and I looked at him but drew complete blanks. "I'm sorry, do we know each other?" I asked.

"Yeah, you was my English teacher."

Leaning over, my husband whispered, "Good job, honey. Good job."

Elizabeth Miller

My Father and Me

December 2005

FROM *700 Sundays*

WHEN I was nine years old, I said to my dad, "Pop, listen. I want to be a comedian. Is that crazy? I want to be a comedian."

He said, "Billy, it's not crazy. And I'm going to help you."

The next day Dad brought home something from his store, the Commodore Music Shop, that started to change my life. It was a tape recorder. It was profound for us because in those days there was no home videotape or anything like that. This was the only way my two brothers and I could hear ourselves back. We could make up our own TV shows and radio shows, practice our imitations. We'd do our shows in the living room for the relatives and hear them back. It was a way to develop our timing.

Dad started showing us the really funny people on television to inspire us. He would let us stay up late on school nights to watch Ernie Kovacs, the great Steve Allen with Tom Poston and Don Knotts and Louie Nye, and the greatest comedian ever to grace television, Sid Caesar.

This is when my uncle Berns really entered our lives, and he would forever change them. A wild one, a Zero Mostel kind of personality, Berns was a mystical man with shoulder-length white hair and a long white beard. He could do magic tricks and mime. He loved to be silly and make people laugh. Everyone was pulled to him, as if he were a magnet.

One day, Dad brought home this record from his shop. It was a Spike Jones record. Spike would have different kinds of sound effects—gunshots, whistles, dog barks—all perfectly integrated into his arrangements. I never heard such crazy stuff in my life. Uncle Berns said, "Lip-synch it and do it for the family." I memorized every moment of "You Always Hurt the One You Love," got it down perfectly, every whistle and scream. They loved it. The living room was my room now.

My brothers and I were always performing for the family. Rip would sing, Joel and I would do something together, and then I'd close the show. It's still the best room I've ever worked. Every family event was an opening night for us. We would get paid with change. My cousin Edith would give me dimes, and I would stick them on my forehead. When my forehead was full, the show was over. Mom and Dad were always the best audience. That's how you start. You want to make your folks laugh.

Often Dad would improvise with us on the tape recorder. It was so great to spend this kind of time with him. As much as I loved playing baseball and watching it, there are other ways of "having a catch."

AND THEN when I was 15, I made a new discovery. I saw The Girl. This wasn't lust. I fell in love with an adorable blond girl. She was the cutest thing I'd ever seen. I knew what head-over-heels meant because I kept tripping and falling when I would follow her home from school.

Finally I got up enough nerve to ask her out and she said yes. Then we really started going out, and it was the first time I made out with somebody in a movie theater. I got up enough nerve and I said, "You know what? I love you, I really do. Let's go steady."

"Oh, no, Billy, I can't do that," she said. "As a matter of fact, I don't want to go out with you anymore. I really just like you as a friend."

"Really?"

The rejection was too much to take. I was mad. I

was embarrassed. I felt like a fool. I was still in love and I was in terrible pain. I couldn't see straight. I remember the day after she dumped me, it was a Tuesday night . . .

OCTOBER 15, 1963. I was sitting at the kitchen table studying for my chemistry test in the morning. I had just lost The Girl. Who cared about chemistry? Was it ever going to be important in my life? Was anyone ever going to say to me, "Billy, what's lead?" And I wouldn't hesitate and look him right in the eye and proudly say, "Pb."

"Yes it is, Bill. Yes, it is. Here's a million dollars."

That was never going to happen. And every time I'd turn a page in the chemistry book, I'd see The Girl's face.

My parents came into the kitchen to say good-bye. They were on their way out to their Tuesday night bowling league. They loved bowling with their friends. They had so much fun doing it. And frankly, this was pretty much the only fun they were having now because times had changed for us, and not for the better.

My father's business had closed a few years earlier. The music shop couldn't keep up with the discount record places that were springing up around Manhattan. My dad was now 54 years old, and he was scared. With Joel and Rip away at college, for the first time he was out of a job.

It was so sad to see him struggle this way. When

he walked into the kitchen that October night he looked worried. He looked upset. And when he saw me pining away for The Girl, he looked mad. We had just finished a month of Sundays together, talking about comedy, watching baseball. With my brothers away at school, I didn't have to share him. It was just the two of us for the first time.

But that night, as I stared at my chemistry book, he started yelling at me. "Billy, look at you. You're going to have to get your grades up. You're going to have to study because I can't afford to send you to school. That's how it's going to work, kid. You understand? You're going to have to get a scholarship or something. Look at you moping around. This is all because of that girl, isn't it?"

I snapped, "What the hell do you know?" It flew out of my mouth. I never spoke to him like that. Ever.

He looked at me, rage in his eyes. I was scared, didn't know what to do.

I froze. He was quiet now, the words measured.

"Don't talk to me like that, please." And he and my mother left.

I felt awful. Oh, why did I say that? I ran after him to apologize, but they were in the car and gone before I could get there. I came back to the kitchen, thinking, Well, they'll be home around 11:30, quarter to twelve. I'll apologize then, and maybe he'll help me study for this test.

Before I got into bed, I closed the door, but not all the way. And I fell asleep.

I WOKE up to the sound of them coming through the front door. I looked at the clock. It was 11:30, just like always. I could hear Mom coming down the hallway toward the back of the house, where the bedrooms were. And as I was waking up, I could hear her, just like always . . . she was laughing.

Or so I thought. I was confused getting out of my sleep. She wasn't laughing at all. She was crying, hysterically, and it got louder and louder.

The door flew open. The light blinded me. "Billy, Billy, Daddy's gone. Daddy's gone. Daddy's gone."

My uncle Danny was with her. They spoke at the same time, but I only heard one thing. "Dad's gone, kid. He didn't have a chance. Dad is dead."

I was confused. I thought they were talking about their father. I said, "Grandpa died?"

Mom held my face tenderly and said, "Billy, no. Listen to me. Dad had a heart attack at the bowling alley. They tried to save him. They couldn't. He's gone. He died there, Billy."

She laid her head on my shoulder. Then she looked at me, her red eyes glistening and said, "Oh, Billy."

AFTER THE funeral, everyone came back to the house. There must have been hundreds of family members, neighbors, friends, and a lot of food and conversation to keep your mind off your loss during the mourning period. It's called a shiva. But to me, the right word is "shiver" because the feeling of Pop's death made me tremble.

This house that was always filled with laughter and jazz was now so sad and dark. I stayed in my room. I didn't come out. I mean, I didn't want to see anybody. Friends would come over to try to talk to me, try to make me feel better, you know. But nobody really knows what to say to you. Hell, we didn't know what to say about a lot of stuff. A living room filled with people, and I didn't care.

And then one day, I heard laughter. Big laughs. Everybody having a great time. I had to come out to see who was working my room. It was my crazy uncle Berns. Performing for the family. He was making everybody laugh. He was so funny even my mother was smiling.

He was carrying on, making everybody else feel a little bit better and taking some of the pain out of his heart as well. Making people forget just for a few moments why they were there, and it was okay.

He had just lost his brother, the person he was closest to in the world. And the message to me was profound, because it meant that even in your worst pain, it's still okay to laugh. 🕊

Credits and Acknowledgements

Joy

"Overtaken by Joy," by Ardis Whitman, *Reader's Digest,* April 1965.

"Shall We Dance?" by Neil Simon. Reprinted with the permission of Simon & Schuster, Inc., from *The Play Goes On* by Neil Simon. Copyright © 1999 Neil Simon.

"The Bottom Line on Happiness," by Clayton M. Christensen. Copyright © 2010 by Harvard Business School Publishing (July 10, 2010).

"Obey That Impulse," by William Moulton Marston. Condensed from a CBS Radio Broadcast, March 18, 1941.

"In Search of Heaven," by Gail Cameron Wescott, *Reader's Digest,* December 2005.

"Gilligan's Aisle," by Jeanne Marie Laskas, © 1996 by Jeanne Marie Laskas. *Washington Post Magazine* (January 7, 1996).

Miracles

"The Gold-and-Ivory Tablecloth," by Rev. Howard C. Schade, *Reader's Digest,* December 1954.

"A Dog Like No Other," by Peter Muilenburg, *Reader's Digest,* June 1998.

"'A Man Don't Know What He Can Do,'" by Elise Miller Davis, *Reader's Digest,* October 1952.

"The Forked Stick Phenomenon," by Emily and Per Ola d'Aulaire, *Reader's Digest,* May 1976.

"Letter in the Wallet," by Arnold Fine, © 1984 by Arnold Fine. *Jewish Press* (January 20, 1984).

Gratitude

"Christopher Reeve's Decision," by Christopher Reeve. Copyright © 1998 Cambria Productions, Inc. From the book *Still Me* by Christopher Reeve, published by Random House, an imprint of Random House Publishing Group, a division of Random House, Inc. Reprinted with permission.

"Information Please," by Paul Villiard, *Reader's Digest,* June 1966.

"The Dream Horse and the Dining-Room Table," by Billy Porterfield. Reprinted with the permission of HarperCollins Publishers, Inc. from *Diddy Waw Diddy* by Billy Porterfield. Copyright © 1994 by Billy Porterfield.

"His Gift of the Future," by Marc Lerner, *Reader's Digest,* June 1995.

"A Heart for the Run," by Gary Paulsen. Excerpted from *Puppies, Dogs, and Blue Northers* by Gary Paulsen. Copyright © 1996 by Gary Paulsen. Used by permission of Houghton Mifflin Harcourt Publishing Company. All rights reserved.

"The Gratitude Club," by Steve Hartman, *Reader's Digest,* July/ August 2012. From the CBS News Archives.

Giving

"The Christmas Present," by James A. Michener, *Reader's Digest,* December 1967.

"The Man on the Train," by Alex Haley, *Reader's Digest,* February 1991.

"Ferragamo's Gift," by Susan Shreve, © 2003 by Susan Richards Shreve. Originally appeared in *MORE* magazine as "Dear Signor Ferragamo." Used by permission of Brandt & Hochman Literary Agents, Inc. All Rights Reserved.

"Letting Go," by Litty Mathew, *Reader's Digest,* December 2009/January 2010.

"She Gave Her Father Life," by Henry Hurt, *Reader's Digest,* November 1996.

Holidays

"A Family for Freddie," by Abbie Blair, *Reader's Digest,* December 1964.

"A String of Blue Beads," by Fulton Oursler, *Reader's Digest,* December 1951.

"Night of Hope and Possibility," by Roxanne Willems Snopek, *Reader's Digest,* December 1999.

"The Holiday I'll Never Forget" ("All I'm Asking For," by Rick Bragg; "The Gift of Possibility," by Esmeralda Santiago; "Eight Candles, Nine Lives," by Melissa Fay Greene; "Sharing the Sweetness," by Tayari Jones; "Some Assembly Required," by Floyd Skloot; "A Legacy of Love," by Lee Smith; "Merry, Silly Christmas," by Jenny Allen), *Reader's Digest,* December 2011/January 2012.

"Christmas Out of Season," by Robert Fulghum. "Christmas in August," from *All I Really Need To Know I Learned In Kindergarten* by Robert L. Fulgham, copyright © 1986, 1988 by Robert L. Fulgham. Used by permission of Villard Books, a division of Random House, Inc.

Healing

"A Love Like No Other," by Skip Hollandsworth. Copyright © 1994 by *Texas Monthly* (February 1994).

"Two Words to Avoid, Two to Remember," by Arthur Gordon, *Reader's Digest,* January 1968. Reprinted with permission by the estate of Arthur Gordon.

"The Day My Silent Brother Spoke," by Jim Watson, *Reader's Digest,* January 1992.

"The Ugliest Cat in the World," by Penny Porter, *Reader's Digest,* March 1993.

"My Fourteenth Summer," by W. W. Meade, *Reader's Digest,* July 1998.

"Mother Courage," by Linda Kramer Jenning, *Reader's Digest,* July 2009.

Heroes

"An Open Letter to Students," by Dwight D. Eisenhower, *Reader's Digest,* October 1948.

"Three Days to See," by Helen Keller, © 1932 By The Helen Keller Foundation Education Program. *The Atlantic Monthly* (January 1933), 77 N. Washington Street, Boston, Massachusetts 02116.

"How America Can Make Brotherhood Work," by Bill Bradley, *Reader's Digest* 75th Anniversary Issue, 1997.

"The Night I Met Einstein," by Jerome Weidman, *Reader's Digest,* November 1955.

"My Father and Me," by Billy Crystal. From *700 Sundays,* copyright © 2005 by Billy Crystal. Published by arrangement with Grand Central Publishing, a Division of Hachette Book Group. New York, NY. All rights reserved.

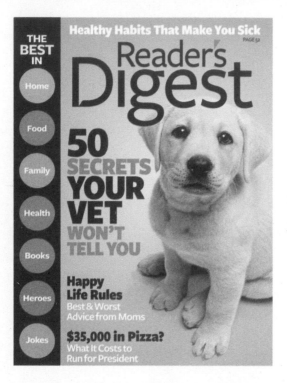

oy Miracles Grat

Healing Heroes Jo

Giving Holidays

cles Gratitude G

Heroes Joy Mirac

Holidays Healing

Gratitude Giving

oes Joy Miracles

ays Healing Her

de Giving Holi